Dispersed Camping and Boondocking
on America's Public Lands

John Soares

Camp for Free: Dispersed Camping and Boondocking on America's Public Lands

Note: Nearly all the material in this book should stay relevant for many, many years. Visit dispersedcamping.net for updated resource recommendations, including websites, apps, and more.

© 2020 by John Soares
Updated for 2022

Published by Get Outside Press (GetOutsidePress.com)

ISBN: 978-0-9999040-0-8

Cover photo: Near Zion National Park, Utah, by Gracie Schmitt
All other photos by the author
Maps courtesy US Forest Service and Bureau of Land Management

ACT RESPONSIBLY: LEAVE NO TRACE

Higher numbers of people doing dispersed camping in recent years has led to increased bad behavior, including driving and camping in forbidden areas, leaving trash, not properly disposing of human waste, and not following campfire rules. This has led officials to restrict dispersed camping in some areas. You must take full responsibility for your actions and the actions of your travel companions: follow Leave No Trace principles and all local regulations. (See "Chapter 6: Dispersed Camping Best Practices.")

DON'T START A WILDFIRE

Most dispersed camping in the United States occurs in the West, which is prone to major wildfires. Make sure you understand how to safely have a campfire and use your camp stove (see "Chapter Six: Dispersed Camping Best Practices"), and always follow current regulations on campfires and stove use. Never drive your vehicle off-road: not only does it cause environmental damage, it can also spark a wildfire. Finally, properly extinguish anything that is burning or hot, from cigarettes to everything else.

SAFETY DISCLAIMER

Dispersed camping and boondocking involve inherent dangers. Weather, natural hazards, road conditions, actions of other people, and the knowledge, skills, and actions of you and your party all affect your safety. This book provides no guarantees of the safety of you and your party: you assume full responsibility, including following all laws.

DEDICATION

For Stephanie Hoffman, my favorite person to travel with anywhere in the world, and especially in the backcountry.

Table of Contents

Introduction

Dispersed camping lets you escape civilization and head out into the wild areas where you can tune in to nature and calm down, far from the bustle and noise of town and city. Best of all, it's free!

Sound good? Then *Camp for Free: Dispersed Camping & Boondocking on America's Public Lands* is for you.

What This Book Is About

This book is about:

1. Choosing the best areas for dispersed camping in the United States
2. Finding the best dispersed camping sites
3. Minimizing your environmental impact while dispersed camping
4. Staying as safe as possible while dispersed camping

What This Book Is NOT About

This book is NOT about:

1. Camping in organized campgrounds. In "Chapter One: Dispersed Camping Defined," I do have a brief discussion of the pros and cons of organized campgrounds and how to make the most of the experience.

2. Identifying specific dispersed camping sites. There are about 640 million acres of federal land in the United States, with hundreds of thousands (perhaps millions) of potential places to park your vehicle or pitch a tent. (My site dispersedcamping.net has a list of websites and apps that do identify some of these places.)

3. Converting a vehicle to make it optimal for travel. That is a complex subject: A wide variety of websites and online videos provide ideas and instructions, plus there are several books on the process.

4. Discussing specifics of brands and types of gear. "Appendix One: What to Take" provides a detailed list of items, and I have a frequently updated list of my recommended camping gear and related items at dispersedcamping.net.

This Book Is for You...

This book is for everyone who wants to head out into America's public lands and camp for free outside of organized campgrounds. You may have a comfortable home and just want to go camping for a couple of nights two to three times per year. You may be travelling for a week or three and want to camp for free as much as possible while you're exploring different places. You may travel in your vehicle for extended periods and you're looking for places you can camp for a week at a time, or longer. You may drive a sedan, an SUV, a truck, a van, or an RV.

Regardless of how often you want to go and what vehicle you drive, you'll find detailed information and advice in this book that will help you find great places for dispersed camping.

A private and beautiful dispersed camping site near Goblin Valley in southern Utah

Boondocking...

Boondocking is part of the title of this book, and for good reason. It's a term that many people are familiar with, and for most, it means dispersed camping in an RV.

However, as explained in more detail in Chapter One: Dispersed Camping Defined, dispersed camping is the broader term that I use throughout the book because it applies to the entire range of camping spots on public lands, not just the small percentage accessible by RVs.

If you have an RV, this book is also for you! All the information applies; you just have to be careful about picking areas and access roads suitable for your rig.

Organization of This Book

The book contains eight chapters with all the important information you need to find the best dispersed camping spots and then enjoy them responsibly and safely.

In "Chapter One: Dispersed Camping Defined," I explain exactly what dispersed camping is, along with related terms like boondocking, primitive camping, and more. The chapter includes a discussion of the pros and cons of dispersed camping, and also the pros and cons of organized campgrounds and RV parks.

In "Chapter Two: Vehicles for Dispersed Camping," I examine the full range of vehicles you could use, and I rank them by most suitable to least suitable.

In "Chapter Three: Where You Can Go Dispersed Camping," I lay out the many broad options available, primarily on national forests and BLM lands, but also on state property and other lands.

In "Chapter Four: Before You Go Dispersed Camping," I cover a wide range of topics, including deciding where and when to go, gathering information, obtaining maps and apps, and ensuring your vehicle is in good shape for the journey.

In "Chapter Five: Finding the Best Dispersed Camping Sites," I provide detailed information about everything you need to do to ensure you find a great site that's suitable for you, your travel companions, and your vehicle.

In "Chapter Six: Dispersed Camping Best Practices," I talk about Leave No Trace principles and related ways you can minimize your impact on the environment.

In "Chapter Seven: Dispersed Camping Safety," I give advice on many important topics, including weather, wildfires, animals, natural hazards, hunters, personal protection, and much more.

In "Chapter Eight: Sleep for Free in Towns and Cities," I discuss various legal options for sleeping in your vehicle in and near populated areas without having to pay, in case you can't make it to government land for dispersed camping in one day.

In the appendix "What to Take," I share a detailed list of the essential items and supplies you need for dispersed camping. Note that there is an updated list of all the items and supplies at dispersedcamping.net.

The Stories

At the end of each chapter you'll find one or more stories. Many are my experiences from when I've traveled alone ("My Story"), some are shared experiences of my travels with my sweetie Stephanie ("Our Story"), and a couple are directly from Stephanie ("Stephanie's Story"). The stories give you a taste of what it's like to experience the many facets of dispersed camping, including the many highs and the occasional lows. Each story finishes with "lessons learned" that help guide you to safer and more enjoyable experiences.

Why My Website DispersedCamping.net Is So Important

On dispersedcamping.net I share a vast amount of different resources, including relevant government agencies, important websites, related YouTube channels, and top recommendations for books, gear, apps, and more.

I have not placed any links to other websites in this book because over time links can change, and some websites simply shut down. Keeping all the key information on dispersedcamping.net allows me to update it frequently and make it as useful as possible to you.

Dispersed Camping: An Invitation...

I've been doing dispersed camping for over 30 years, the first sixteen years by myself, and the last 14 years and counting with my sweetheart Stephanie usually by my side. We find secluded and beautiful spots all over the western United States where we can relax and enjoy both the wilderness and each other's company.

This book is your free ticket to America's beautiful outdoors. Join me in the pages ahead to find out exactly what dispersed camping is all about, and how you can make the most of it.

My Story: A Recent Dispersed Camping Trip

I earn royalties from my hiking guidebooks on Northern California (see northerncaliforniahikingtrails.com), but the bulk of my income comes from writing projects I do for businesses and nonprofits.

In the summer of 2019, I had a big project writing lecture outlines and test questions for a college-level California history textbook. I find that I focus much better when I'm out dispersed camping because I have none of the distractions of modern life, especially the Internet. So I decided to head out alone for a week into the beautiful mountains west of Mount Shasta in far Northern California to camp, hike, and get some work done.

I loaded up the Kia Sedona minivan and drove to a special dispersed camping spot Stephanie and I had discovered the summer before. It's secluded and near a small stream bordered by meadows and flowers, with plenty of tall pines and firs to provide shade for my writing table. The narrow dirt road continues on for another mile past the camping spot, with smaller roads branching off, perfect for local nature walks.

Every day from early morning to early afternoon I concentrated on my writing, with birds and squirrels the only distraction. In the afternoons I hiked the dirt roads and also spent time watching the water tumble over small boulders in the creek, identifying wildflowers, and gazing up at the steep surrounding mountains. One afternoon I climbed cross-country high up to the spine of a ridge, with a vista of Mount Shasta as my reward.

On the sixth morning I moved on. After a long day hike on the Pacific Crest Trail, I drove one of the major dirt roads in the area for several miles, stopping for an early dinner along a section of the road with a full view of the jagged peaks of the nearby Trinity Alps. A little farther along I took a side road and quickly found an excellent level spot in a small clearing. Just before sunset I took a short walk; the last rays of the sun lit up the lichens on the red fir trunks, turning them a luminescent light green, while the same rays burnished nearby Mount Eddy burnt red.

The main dirt road near my campsite, just before sunset

The next day I hiked the Pacific Crest Trail through forest and meadows to the Deadfall Lakes, and then on up to the summit of Mount Eddy. This is one of the premier hikes in

Introduction

the region, with a jaw-dropping view of Mount Shasta, the Trinity Alps, and countless other mountains stretching to the far horizon in all directions.

In the early evening I drove to an area a Forest Service employee had told me about. Here a dirt road winds through an open valley bounded by metamorphic mountains. On this last night I stood for an hour under the brilliantly clear sky looking at the Milky Way and the myriad stars, interrupted only by a few meteors.

The next morning, refreshed and energized by my time in the wild, I returned home, ready again for more civilized life, but already planning my next dispersed camping trip.

Lessons Learned

1. Dispersed camping is the perfect way to get away from civilization. It calms the mind and allows you to focus more deeply on whatever you want. On this trip, it was a mix of work and immersion in the natural beauty of creeks, forests, mountains, and sky.

2. It's important to do pre-trip planning (much more about this in "Chapter Three: Where You Can Go Dispersed Camping" and "Chapter Four: Before You Go Dispersed Camping"). Of the three places I camped, I'd been to the first one before and a Forest Service employee told me about the last one. I only had to search for the second one, and I already knew it was in an area with many possibilities.

Chapter One

Dispersed Camping Defined

In this first chapter I discuss just exactly what I mean by dispersed camping, how the term boondocking is similar, and why I choose to use the term "dispersed camping" rather than "boondocking." I also discuss the pros and cons of traditional campgrounds, RV parks, and dispersed camping itself.

Dispersed Camping and Boondocking

Fundamentally, this book is about "dispersed camping." As defined by the United States Forest Service, dispersed camping:

1. Takes place on public lands (Forest Service, Bureau of Land Management, and other federal and state lands)

2. Costs nothing (however, in a few jurisdictions you'll have to buy a permit just to be on the land)

3. Occurs outside of organized campgrounds (and usually far away from them)

4. Offers no amenities (no toilets, no tables, no water, no nothing)

5. Is subject to rules and regulations that vary from jurisdiction to jurisdiction

Dispersed Camping Defined

"Boondocking" is a term most commonly used in the RV community. Boondocking is a type of dispersed camping, but it usually refers to dispersed camping in places accessible to RVs. Boondocking sites are accessed by wider roads that are in good shape, and they have enough space for big rigs to turn around.

However, the overwhelming majority of dispersed camping sites lie down dirt roads that are narrow and rougher, some requiring high clearance and AWD/4WD. These roads are not suitable for most RVs, especially the larger ones.

Therefore, dispersed camping is the more general term, and dispersed camping is the term I use in this book. But, if you have an RV and want to "boondock," this book still has plenty of information for you!

Other Commonly Used Terms

There are several terms you'll frequently see that are related to dispersed camping.

Free Camping

This means exactly what it says: you pay nothing to camp. This includes dispersed camping, of course, but it also includes a number of actual campgrounds in more remote places that don't charge. These campgrounds often have tables, toilets, fire pits, and water.

Primitive Camping

The term "primitive camping" can mean the same thing as dispersed camping, but the term can also refer to campgrounds with few amenities: for example, sites may have a table and a fire pit, but there is no potable water and no toilets. These campgrounds may or may not charge a fee.

Remote Camping

Another term with multiple definitions, remote camping basically means camping far away from organized campgrounds. It's a broad term that can include dispersed camping and primitive camping.

Dry Camping

At its most basic, dry camping means no supplied water. This describes virtually all dispersed camping sites, plus many of the primitive/remote sites.

Wild Camping

Wild camping is a term used almost exclusively in Europe. It refers to camping outside of organized campgrounds, usually for free.

How I Chose the Title of the Book

I put a lot of thought into it. There are all those terms above, some of which have different meanings to different people. Fundamentally, though, this book is about how to find and enjoy dispersed campsites that are free. And, as explained above, boondocking is a very common term that many people know that is essentially a restricted type of dispersed camping. Thus the title:

Camp for Free: Dispersed Camping & Boondocking on America's Public Lands

Again, keep in mind that I'll use the term "dispersed camping" throughout the book, although much of what I say also applies to RV folks who "boondock."

Why Do Dispersed Camping?

I've been doing dispersed camping for most of my adult life (see "My Story: All My Vehicles" at the end of "Chapter Two: Vehicles for Dispersed Camping") and I think it's a far better experience than staying in campgrounds (or RV parks). Here's what I love about it, and why I think you will love it also.

A More Wild Experience

Wherever you find your special camping spot, whether it's in the red-rock desert in northern Arizona, or in the high mountains of Wyoming or California, you'll be surrounded by nature in all directions. Cliffs and peaks, trees and flowers—and a dark sky at night so you can watch the stars slowly turn, with the occasional meteor flash.

Quiet at Night

It's usually easy to find an excellent dispersed camping spot that's far away from anyone else: The nearest person may actually be miles away. So you won't hear music blaring, people shouting, generators roaring, or doors slamming.

What will you hear at night? The wind in the trees. Perhaps an owl calling in the dark. Occasionally a coyote or three.

Much easier to sleep! And, of course, it's quiet in the day, too—just the sounds of nature.

Solitude

Most of us spend much of our lives in close proximity to other people, usually lots and lots of other people. Dispersed camping allows you to be alone with your thoughts, to let your brain, body, and spirit calm down. You'll likely find that the solitude helps you think more clearly about what you want in life, and that you're better able to make life decisions, large and small.

Traveling with others? Sharing a special spot in the wilderness can bring you closer, allowing for deeper communication and deeper connection. And you'll also be sharing experiences and building life-time memories.

Room to Roam

Wherever you are, there are places to explore starting right from your camp. Just about everywhere you'll find dirt roads and perhaps trails, allowing you to go for miles if you wish. In the desert Southwest? You can usually roam cross-country over the open land.

It's Free!

What's your cost? Almost always it's exactly zero dollars. This lifestyle is perfect if you're on a budget and need to stretch your money.

Advantages of Organized Campgrounds

Organized campgrounds can be great. I haven't stayed in all that many in my life, but they do have their perks:

-- Picnic tables that make it easy to cook and sit and eat
-- Flat areas to pitch a tent
-- Fire pits and/or barbecues
-- Potable water
-- Toilets
-- Showers (maybe)
-- Often near beautiful scenery
-- Often near recreational opportunities such as hiking trails and lakes for boating and swimming
-- Opportunities to meet interesting people and make new friends

Disadvantages of Organized Campgrounds

And, of course, there are the many downsides of organized campgrounds.

Noise

Campgrounds can be very, very noisy. Not only do you hear barking dogs, vehicle engines, and perhaps generators, along with normal conversations, but it's unfortunately all too common to hear loud music and people shouting and partying. Stephanie and I camped at the Bridalveil Creek Campground near Glacier Point in Yosemite National Park for two nights several years ago. Both nights people in an adjacent site stayed up late talking and laughing around a campfire, and both nights there was at least one nearby group in the campground that partied all night, including drunken yelling.

Now, it's not always the case that there's a lot of noise. But there will be significant noise during the day and evening as people live their lives outside, even if they're being considerate. You can't help but hear them.

Campfire Smoke

Campgrounds often actively encourage people to have campfires by selling firewood. Frequently the smoke hugs the ground and completely fills the campground, meaning everyone has to breathe it in. Not fun and not healthy.

Lack of Privacy

You can easily have a couple dozen people within 30-40 feet of you, especially in campgrounds with sites packed right next to each other. You hear them talking, you hear them preparing their food, you hear their bodily noises. And they hear you too, of course.

Dispersed Camping Defined

It Costs Money

And frequently some serious money. Some campgrounds are still inexpensive at $10-20 per night, but others now cost $35-$40 per night. More and more campgrounds require you to reserve ahead of time online, and that usually means paying a "convenience fee" on top of the per-night rate.

If you camp for a month at an average of 30 dollars a night, you'll be out at least 900 bucks.

RV Parks: Pros and Cons

Some of you travel in RVs. RV parks share most of the advantages and disadvantages of campgrounds. There are also substantial benefits to RV parks:

-- Water
-- Electricity
-- Sewage
-- Showers
-- Laundry facilities
-- Wi-Fi (maybe)
-- Cable television (maybe)
-- Other amenities, such as a recreation room (maybe)
-- Proximity to stores and restaurants

RV parks also have downsides:

-- They are more likely to be located in or near towns and/or beside major highways, which means more noise, more air pollution, and less nature.

-- You will typically be packed very close to your neighbors.

-- They can be noisy, especially when people run generators.

Potential Downsides to Dispersed Camping

Throughout my long history of dispersed camping, I've had almost uniformly positive experiences, and so have my many friends and acquaintances.

However, not everything about dispersed camping is sunshine and flowers all the time. Here are some of the challenges you could face. Later chapters in this book discuss in detail how to deal with all of these challenges, but for now let's examine them briefly.

You Have to Bring Everything with You

Not only does your dispersed camping spot lack the basic amenities of a campground, you are frequently far from civilization, including food stores and restaurants, and also water sources.

So you have to bring all of the food you will need for the entire time, and, just as importantly, you have to bring plenty of water for drinking, cleaning, and washing your body. In addition, you need to make sure you bring everything else you need, because stores are often a long way off.

No Toilets

Your vehicle may be equipped with a toilet, but many vehicles are not, so many dispersed campers go outside. Not a big deal for most people, but a bit of an issue for some.

No Showers

Yes, if you have an RV or conversion van you have a shower, but many dispersed campers travel in smaller vehicles without one. Staying clean—or clean enough—can be one of the challenges of dispersed camping. You can purchase portable showers, and if the weather is warm enough and there's deep water in a nearby stream or lake, you can go swimming. You can also clean yourself with a moist towel, or do what I frequently do: use water from gallon jugs.

Less Chance of Help

Being out in the boonies means it can be more difficult to get help, whether medical help if you get sick or injured, or mechanical help if your vehicle breaks down. In addition, cell phone reception can be spotty or nonexistent in some remote areas.

Bad weather

Weather happens. If you're out camping and it rains for three days, you'll be spending a lot of time holed up in your vehicle (or staying in your tent). (Of course, this same issue affects all travelers.)

Often you can plan trips around bad weather, but sometimes you can't. You either have a certain time period for traveling, or you're traveling long-term and you can't avoid the weather. I did the majority of my van vagabonding with Hana and Molly, my two golden retrievers. They were great companions, but a little less so when they were wet and muddy from being out in the rain.

Fear

Some people, especially those new to camping, get scared to varying degrees by worrying about the various critters that could get them (human and other), or other bad things that could happen. Most of these concerns are very unlikely to occur, of course, and there's a lot you can do to prevent and deal with anything that does happen. So the fear is irrational for the most part, but that doesn't mean some people don't feel it.

However, for nearly everyone the fear quickly subsides. Once you get used to sleeping in your vehicle (or a tent), you'll likely find that you sleep even better than you do in a bed in a house.

Getting Lost

Getting lost is a valid concern, either when you're driving or when you're exploring on foot or bike. Techniques for knowing where you are and where you are going are addressed in detail in "Chapter Five: Finding the Best Dispersed Camping Sites," and "Chapter Seven: Dispersed Camping Safety."

Not Sure? Just Try It!

First, read the rest of this book and be sure you've absorbed the most relevant information, including deciding where to go and how to make sure you can actually get there when you want to go.

Second, pick a place that's easy and close by, a place you can do with your current vehicle and current camping equipment. (Alternatively, you may also be able to borrow a friend's or family member's vehicle and camping equipment.)

Third, go. Check it out and see if you like it!

Most people do like it, and they find that they like it more the more they do it. Many grow to love it, just like I do.

Stephanie's Story: Sometimes a Traditional Campground Rocks!

After a couple of weeks of dispersed camping, John and I drove by Kodachrome Basin State Park in Southern Utah: the vistas in the area were pure perfection! The best views were inside the park and, without too much discussion, we decided to spend the night (seeing a sign for hot showers and a laundromat, honestly, was more the deciding factor than the exquisite rock formations.)

Once we paid for a space and were told the campground rules, we parked our van and headed for the trails. We were blown away by the beauty of the sedimentary rock layers, and even more surprised by how few people were out hiking.

Stephanie enjoys a beautiful vista in Kodachrome Basin State Park

After a full day of hiking, exploring, laughing, eating, and loving life, we realized hey, we can actually get clean! We headed to the showers with a fistful of quarters to feed the greedy water meters, expecting the usual: a shower stall where wearing flipflops was a must. As a woman, I expected the showers to be crowded with many ladies waiting as others took their time under the warm water. To my surprise, there was no one waiting for a shower, and best of all it was almost spa-like conditions! Beautifully tiled floors and walls (and they were super clean), large stalls (even enough room to hang your towel so it wouldn't get wet), and plenty of benches in case you had to wait for a free stall. I could go on and on; however, I won't because I need to tell you about the laundromat!

Again, we were so surprised when we entered the laundromat: only one other person and five washers and dryers to choose from. The building was stylish and the inside was quite large with a picnic table and chairs. We brought a bunch of change, thinking that since it was the only laundromat within probably a 50-mile radius, it would cost an arm and a leg just to do one load. Wrong again! It was less than $4.00 to wash and dry our clothes. Unbelievable!

We typically avoid organized campgrounds in large part because of the people noise; yet this place was nearly silent (we totally lucked out!). The other campers were quiet and respectful, and it was very interesting to find out where they were from and the adventures they recently had in Southern Utah. By staying in the campground, we had deeper connections with people because we actually had time to chat, unlike the perfunctory "hello" when you pass someone on a hiking trail.

Who knew that the promise of a hot shower and clean clothes would lead to a great decision? We were so glad that we took the chance and stayed at Kodachrome Basin State Park.

Lessons Learned

1. Staying in an organized campground is a great way to break up the trip, especially for modern conveniences like a

bathroom with running water (and the opportunity to actually sit while doing your biz… ladies you know what I'm talking about!), and, in this case, a hot shower and a laundromat.

2. Most importantly, choose wisely. We didn't read online reviews because we hadn't planned on stopping and there was no cell service. We asked the ranger if we could drive into the park to help us decide if we wanted to stay or not. While driving through, we paid special attention to how close the sites were to each other and how mellow it was overall. In this case, it sealed the deal.

Chapter Two

Vehicles for Dispersed Camping

Your vehicle has a big impact on where you can do dispersed camping and how much comfort you'll have when you're out there. This chapter examines the pros and cons of various types of vehicles for getting into the backcountry.

Why is the choice of vehicle so important? First, what you drive determines which dirt roads you can travel as you search for both camp sites and places to explore; here the important factors are length, width, clearance, and, in especially steep terrain, engine power. In addition, four-wheel-drive or all-wheel-drive can be crucial for situations where the road surface is either very muddy or has deep dirt or sand, but overall, clearance is far more important.

Second, what you drive determines how comfortable you'll be once you've found a site. You'll be most comfortable in a vehicle with enough room for all your stuff, plus a comfy bed that allows you to stretch out fully. Tent camping is definitely less comfortable and requires substantially more time to set up camp, plus you're far more impacted by weather.

Of course, many of us only have one vehicle and we have to use it for dispersed camping, regardless of its limitations. If this is your case, jump to the bottom of the chapter and read "Making Do With the Vehicle You Have."

What follows is an examination of the main types of vehicles people use for dispersed camping, with important considerations if you're contemplating buying another vehicle in the near future. Of course, if you have to use the vehicle for daily driving, you need to take that into account as well.

As we go through the choices, remember the two main criteria mentioned above:

1. The ability to navigate dirt roads of varying conditions
2. The level of comfort you'll have at your dispersed camping site

In addition, factor in how often you'll be dispersed camping and in what types of terrain (mountains, hills, forest, desert) and climate (hot, cold, sun, rain, snow).

Finally, cost is an important factor for most of us.

Here's the list, from the overall best to the overall worst, in my humble opinion (and trust me, opinions definitely differ on this!).

Full-Size Van

This is the best overall choice. Most vans have decent clearance, and most are small enough to handle most dirt roads.

A full-size van also has plenty of room for a bed, with options for tricking out the van with a sink, stove, and other amenities, including a toilet. And it's possible to find vans that have both high clearance and four-wheel-drive, allowing you to go almost anywhere.

Truck with Camper Shell

This can be an excellent option. Many trucks have high clearance and four-wheel-drive, which make them overall the best of all vehicles on dirt roads, thus giving you the widest range of places to explore and camp.

A camper shell provides the basics of shelter and a place to store all your stuff. Some larger camper shells even have small sinks and gas stoves, making life a bit easier.

And when you're back home, you might be able to remove the camper shell (depending on the type of shell and other factors) and then save a bit on gas mileage when using your truck for daily use.

There is one downside to a truck with a camper shell. You have to go outside every time you want to go from the camper shell to the main cab of the vehicle. This isn't necessarily a big deal, but it can be a bit of hassle when it's rainy and muddy outside. There's also a bit of a safety consideration. With most of the options described here (full-size vans, minivans, RVs, SUVs), you can go directly from bed to the driver's seat and quickly drive away if something happens outside that makes you feel unsafe.

Minivan

Stephanie and I currently own a moderately customized Kia Sedona minivan and use it for both dispersed camping and general use.

Minivans are a popular compromise for people looking to balance the basic needs of dispersed camping with having a vehicle that also works well for driving in daily life.

Minivans can make it on the main dirt roads you'll encounter on national forest and BLM Lands that have the most dispersed camping options, and many of the lesser roads, too. They don't have the clearance of many SUVs and trucks, but they have enough to successfully negotiate most bumps and dips and smaller rocks.

Our 2010 Kia Sedona at a primo dispersed campsite

Minivans can be converted for living with a modest amount of effort. Take out the back seats, put in a platform, add your bedding for sleep, and store your stuff in bins underneath the platform (that's what we did), or make it even more elaborate, especially if you travel and camp alone and don't need as much sleeping space, or if you spend a lot of time camping.

SUV

SUVs have nearly the same advantages as trucks regarding the ability to negotiate a wide variety of dirt roads. Although clearance is an issue with many models, nearly all have four-wheel-drive.

Except for the largest models, SUVs can be quite crowded for sleeping, but it definitely can be done. If you're tent camping, though, this is not a factor.

Car

Regular passenger cars, like a four-door sedan, typically have only modest clearance. This means your choice of roads is limited, but you can still go a lot of places.

If your car is big enough, or you are small enough, you can sleep in it, although you may be cramped and you may not be able to stretch out fully, and that's why most people in cars use tents. You also have less room to store everything, which makes organizing and using your stuff more difficult and time consuming.

One big upside: you likely already own the car, so you don't have to get a different vehicle.

8'x8' tent at a dispersed campsite in Northern California

RV

The main downside with RVs is that they are both long and wide, which makes navigating many of the smaller dirt roads impossible. There are significant dispersed camping (boondocking) opportunities in the flatter desert areas on BLM land in the Southwest, but you definitely want to do your homework first and make sure you know the roads you want to travel are suitable for your RV (see "Chapter Five: Finding the Best Dispersed Camping Sites"). RVs in the mountainous areas of the country are a dicey proposition, but there are still options.

The upside to RVs, and it's a big one, is that you have all the conveniences of home: stove, refrigerator, sink, toilet, shower, comfy bed, lots of storage, places to sit, heating and cooling, plus enough room to have a bit of separation from your travel companions.

The smallest RV, and the one most suitable for getting around off pavement, is the Class B. These are also known as sleeper vans and camper vans. Next in Size is the Class C, which looks like a truck in the front. The largest is the Class A; these look like buses and are just as long.

Travel Trailer, Fifth Wheel, Popup Trailer

These three are all similar in that they are attached to the back of your vehicle, usually via a tow connection of some sort. They have many (or even all) of the conveniences of RVs described above, and they also have similar problems of impeded maneuverability.

You'll need a vehicle (truck or SUV, most likely) that's powerful enough to tow it. One advantage: once you find a camping spot, you can unhook your living quarters and use your vehicle to explore farther.

Motorcycle

With the right motorcycle (not the big street machines), you can go almost anywhere, including narrow and overgrown roads that no vehicle would attempt.

Of course, you can't bring much stuff with you, and you're exposed to the elements except when you're in your tent.

Buying a Vehicle?

First, make sure it's likely to be reliable. You don't want your vehicle to break down way in the back of beyond where a tow truck or a mobile mechanic has difficulty reaching you.

Reliability depends on make, model, age, mileage, prior use, and prior maintenance. Do online research and ask people you trust for the best years and models of your vehicle of choice. And always have a good mechanic give the vehicle a thorough inspection before you buy it. Many auto repair shops provide this service and have a checklist of dozens of items; they give you a printout at the end with all problems highlighted.

Buy the best vehicle that you can afford that meets your overall needs. In general, the more you pay, the more life the vehicle will have and the fewer repairs it will need over time.

If you're buying a new or newer vehicle, be aware that dispersed camping will get it dirty and perhaps a bit scratched. When I bought my Subaru Outback brand-new in 2001, I imagined what it would look like after I'd driven it all over the backcountry of the western United States for 10 years with two golden retrievers. This helped me relax and accept the inevitable.

Making Do With the Vehicle You Have

You definitely do not have to buy another vehicle to enjoy dispersed camping. You just have to make sure you choose places suitable for your vehicle (see "Chapter Four: Before You Go Dispersed Camping," and "Chapter Five: Finding the Best Dispersed Camping Sites") and you have to be willing to deal with the realities of your situation.

For example, if you have a passenger car, you can travel the better dirt roads until you find a good spot, and then set up your tent. You can sit in your car and be dry and away from insects when it's raining or buggy, and you can still bring all the things you need to be comfortable. Of course, it's not as cushy as having a van, but it's still very enjoyable.

Converting Your Vehicle for Living/Dispersed Camping

Search Amazon for books and especially YouTube for videos that give detailed advice on how to convert a specific type of vehicle to maximize space and storage for you and all your stuff. Also visit dispersedcamping.net for recommended books and websites. You will be amazed at the amount of information out there, especially for minivans and full-size vans, but also for other vehicles like SUVs.

My Story: All My Vehicles

It doesn't qualify as official dispersed camping, but I slept outside on public lands when I spent a year in my mid-twenties hitchhiking throughout Europe with a backpack. I did stay in quite a few youth hostels, but I also frequently slept outside in forests, fields, and parks.

My first official experiences with dispersed camping occurred in my late 20s. My father died suddenly of a heart attack while traveling to Alaska in his pickup truck with a small camper shell. I flew to Prince Rupert, British Columbia, and then hitchhiked to Hyder, Alaska to retrieve the truck. My dad had all his stuff in the camper shell in the back of the truck, including a sleeping platform.

Although it was definitely emotional driving and camping in my father's truck so soon after he died, I decided to honor his adventurous spirit by making the most of the journey back to Northern California. I spent three weeks wandering through British Columbia, Alberta, Idaho, Washington, and Oregon, visiting beautiful natural areas on the way, and driving down dirt roads in national forests in both countries to find isolated places to camp in the wild. I relished the solitude and the quiet, and the sense of freedom. I also liked that it was free!

In the early 1990s I traveled all over Northern California in my Nissan Sentra to research the trails for my guidebook *100 Classic Hikes: Northern California*. I frequently did dispersed camping with my small tent and sleeping bag, especially in the remoter areas of the Sierra Nevada, Klamath Mountains, and Cascade Range.

However, I realized that I didn't like the hassle of setting up the tent every night, and it was especially a drag when it was any combination of rainy, windy, or cold. Thoughts of more suitable vehicles began percolating through my brain, vehicles I could sleep in comfortably.

I lived on the island of Kaua'i for three years in the late 1990s. I totally loved the climate, lushness, and especially the warm ocean, but I eventually missed my beloved Northern California and the rest of the western United States too much.

I decided I wanted to live in a full-size van and travel throughout the West, exploring new areas as I continued my career as a freelance writer. Fortuitously, near the time I was ready to move back to the mainland, a friend on Kaua'i decided to sell his Ford Econoline 150. He'd already put in a large sleeping platform with drawers underneath, and also four small sliding windows with screens.

I had the van shipped to the mainland, and then I flew to the San Francisco Bay Area with my two golden retrievers, Hana and Molly. I initially stayed at my brother Eric's place for a week or so while I bought a foam pad, a sleeping bag, a cooler, a gas stove, and all the other stuff I needed. I also had a deep-cycle battery installed so that I would have extra power to run lights, my computer, and other electrical appliances.

Then began my most extensive period of both traveling and dispersed camping. Hana, Molly, and I took off in early March to begin a grand journey that lasted into late October. First we headed south into the deserts of Southern California before moving on to Southern Arizona and then swinging up into Southern Utah. I usually had no problem finding an excellent dispersed camping spot on BLM or National Forest land, and it was during this time that I honed my skills for finding the best sites.

As the weather warmed, we continued to the Sierra Nevada of California, and then farther north to the Mount Shasta area, where we spent most of the summer. I found good spots to park at night in the surrounding Shasta-Trinity National Forest, and we made several longer explorations farther into the wilder areas of Northern California, and on up into Oregon. After spending the winter renting a small house in Chico, California, we followed a similar travel pattern and timetable the next year.

The Ford Econoline van

By now I was hooked on the freedom of traveling cheaply and sleeping for free on America's public lands. I had my systems down, plus all my equipment, all of which formed the basis of what I share here in this book, with all the

Vehicles for Dispersed Camping

necessary updates for the computer/internet/cell phone age we live in now.

In 2000 I rented a house in Crescent City, California and then bought a house in rural Del Norte County in 2002. I kept the van and used it for short camping trips, but the van started developing problems that would be very expensive to fix. In short, it was near the end of its life.

Morning view from one of my favorite dispersed camping sites off Hole-in-the-Rock Road, Grand Staircase-Escalante National Monument

So I had to choose another vehicle. This time I made a compromise that I felt best encompassed my needs for a reliable vehicle for daily driving and also the ability to still get into the wild for hiking and dispersed camping: I bought a brand-new Subaru Outback. It was a major downsize from the van, which I donated to a charity.

The Outback got much better mileage than the van, it was far more fun to drive, and it allowed me to get to a few places that the van couldn't, including some of the best dispersed camping sites I ever found.

The Outback: sleeping bag on the diagonal, clothes on the left, ice chest on the right, and all the other stuff unseen in the front seat.

I was able to fold down the back seats to create a flat sleeping area, but it wasn't long enough for me to fully stretch out, so I always slept on the diagonal. While Hana and Molly were still alive, one slept in the front passenger seat and the other slept near my legs; there wasn't much room for my stuff, which I usually put in the driver's seat and on the floor of the passenger seat.

The Outback served me admirably for 18 years and 200,000 miles as I lived primarily in the Mount Shasta area of Northern California (where I met my sweetheart Stephanie) and then in Ashland in southern Oregon. But it was too small for both Stephanie and me to sleep in, so we always took a tent when we did dispersed camping. We began planning the next vehicle and the next phase of traveling and exploring.

We decided that a minivan was the best compromise for us. We needed a vehicle in which we could both sleep comfortably, and that could carry all of our food, equipment, and supplies, plus would get good mileage and be suitable for daily driving needs when we weren't traveling.

But exactly which minivan? The Toyota Sienna is the gold standard of minivans, and it's the one that's by far the favorite of active families, plus people who want a minivan for travelling and dispersed camping.

We spent three months looking for a Sienna in our area, but we didn't find one that had the right combination we wanted: less than 10 years old, less than 100,000 miles, and at a price we were willing to pay.

And then I saw an ad on Craigslist for a 2010 Kia Sedona, one of the less-common minivans. It had only 83,000 miles, and it was less than half the price of what a 2010 Sienna with the same mileage would be. Initially a rental, it had had only one owner since, and she had driven it gently and had taken good care of it. I paid a top-notch mechanic to give it a thorough inspection, which it passed with flying colors. We bought it!

We took all the seats out of the back and hired a good friend to put in a wooden platform. We have room for a big cooler, a small gas stove, plenty of food, and all of our clothes and supplies under the platform, and we have a super-comfy foam pad with a rectangular sleeping bag on top of the platform. We bring our pillows from our bed at home and we sleep great.

Stephanie and I in the back of the "Hotel Sedona"

We've since taken extensive trips in the "Hotel Sedona" to the deserts of Southern California, the Southwest, and the mountains of Northern California and Oregon, almost exclusively doing dispersed camping every night. We love finding a beautiful spot in the wild, spending time outside when we want, and then staying warm and cozy inside the rest of the time.

We're open to yet another vehicle "down the road," especially if we ever decide to travel for months at a time. If so, it would almost certainly be a full-size van with more extensive enhancements.

Lessons Learned

1. It's definitely possible to enjoy dispersed camping with any vehicle, even if it's a small sedan and you sleep in a tent.

2. It's important to buy the best vehicle you can afford that offers the best combination of comfort and ability to navigate dirt roads.

Chapter Three

Where You Can Go Dispersed Camping

This chapter examines both where you can do dispersed camping in a broad sense, and also the typical rules for dispersed camping. Note that "Chapter Five: Finding the Best Dispersed Camping Sites" provides the detailed steps you'll take when you have chosen the general area where you want to go dispersed camping.

Public Lands

You will almost always be camping on public lands. Public lands are mostly owned by the federal government, with a much smaller percentage owned by state governments, and a tiny percentage by local governments.

Public lands are your lands, which means you have a right to use and enjoy them. A variety of different departments and agencies manage public lands, and they have different though partially overlapping missions. However, all of them seek to preserve and protect nature and natural resources while also allowing recreation and extraction and use of resources (principally timber, minerals, and cattle grazing).

These are the principal government agencies and types of agencies that manage lands suitable for dispersed camping:

-- United States Forest Service (and United States Grasslands)
-- Bureau of Land Management
-- National Monuments, National Preserves, National Recreation Areas
-- Wildlife Management Areas (federal and state)
-- State Forests

More details on each are below, plus info on less common dispersed camping options.

Dispersed Camping: It's Best in the West

The West hosts the most spots for dispersed camping. What do I mean by the West? It's the twelve states from the Pacific Coast to the Rocky Mountains:

-- California
-- Oregon
-- Washington
-- Idaho
-- Montana
-- Wyoming
-- Colorado
-- Utah
-- Nevada
-- Arizona
-- New Mexico
-- Texas

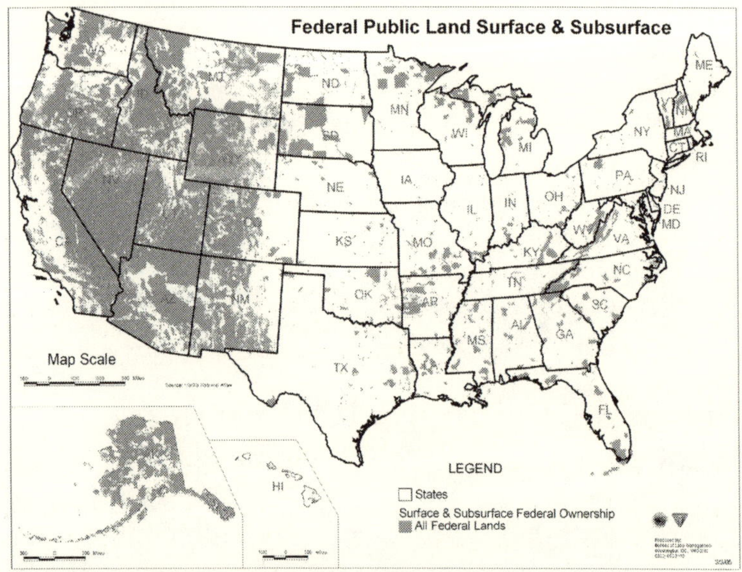

Federal public lands in the United States. Not all of this land is available for dispersed camping.

What About the Rest of the Country?

There are definitely opportunities for dispersed camping east of the Rocky Mountains, mostly in national forests and on national grasslands, but they are more limited. Whereas travelers in much of the rural West will frequently have nearby lands available for camping, that is not the case outside of the West. Most of the dispersed camping spots are in national forests, primarily in the Appalachian Mountains and in the Upper Midwest.

Typical Rules

Rules vary by specific national forest, BLM district, or other entity. However, none of them let you do dispersed camping indefinitely at a single site. Usually you can stay only a certain number of days at a given site (often 14 days), before you have to move at least a certain distance away to another site (typically 5-25 miles). In addition, there is usually a limit to the total number of days you can spend on a given national forest, BLM district, or other entity in a calendar year, with 30 days the common maximum.

Other rules specify how far you should be from a water source (at least 100 feet and frequently 200 feet or more) and how far you need to be from developed areas and sometimes certain roads. The rules also give specifics of a dispersed campsite and proper practices, like using existing sites and fire rings, not parking in meadows or wet areas, practicing Leave No Trace principles, and more. For an in-depth discussion, see "Chapter Six: Dispersed Camping Best Practices."

These rules are designed to allow more people to enjoy dispersed camping and to minimize the impact of campers on the land. You are responsible for knowing the specific regulations for where you are going, so make sure you do your research before heading down a dirt road to camp. Check the agency website and also call or stop by to make sure you have the details. Doing this also allows you to get detailed advice on the best places to do dispersed camping, and if there are specific areas you should avoid. (See

"Chapter Four: Before You Go Dispersed Camping," and "Chapter Five: Finding the Best Dispersed Camping Sites.")

Note: the increased risk of severe wildfires has led to bans on dispersed camping from late summer into fall in some areas, especially in national forests in the West. Always check with the relevant governing agency!

United States Forest Service

The Department of the Interior began managing publicly owned forests in 1891. Legislation passed in 1905 created the United States Forest Service (USFS). Its mission and functions have shifted over the years; now the USFS, a branch of the Department of Agriculture, tries to balance wilderness preservation, recreation, timber harvesting, mining, and grazing, not always to the approval of everyone.

National Forests and National Grasslands

The USFS controls 193 million acres distributed across 154 national forests and 20 grasslands. Most Forest Service lands are—no surprise—forested, and are typically located in mountainous terrain, mostly in the West, as stated above. By contrast, the 20 national grasslands lie in the Great Plains east of the Rocky Mountains, stretching from North Dakota down to Texas. The national grasslands are flat to rolling—a perfect place to enjoy the open sky, especially at night.

Bureau of Land Management

Created in 1946, the Bureau of Land Management (BLM) brought several preexisting federal land agencies under the control of a single agency. BLM controls 247 million acres (by far the majority of public lands), virtually all of it in the West. Much of the terrain is desert and semidesert, and as such was considered unsuitable for homesteading in the nineteenth century, thus keeping it in public hands.

Like the Forest Service, BLM has a multifaceted mission that includes wilderness preservation, recreation, timber harvesting, mining, and grazing. And, like the Forest Service, it is often criticized by environmentalists for putting too much emphasis on resource use and extraction; some detractors call it the Bureau of Logging and Mining, an unfair characterization given the often-conflicting directives given to the BLM by Congress, the executive branch, and the court system.

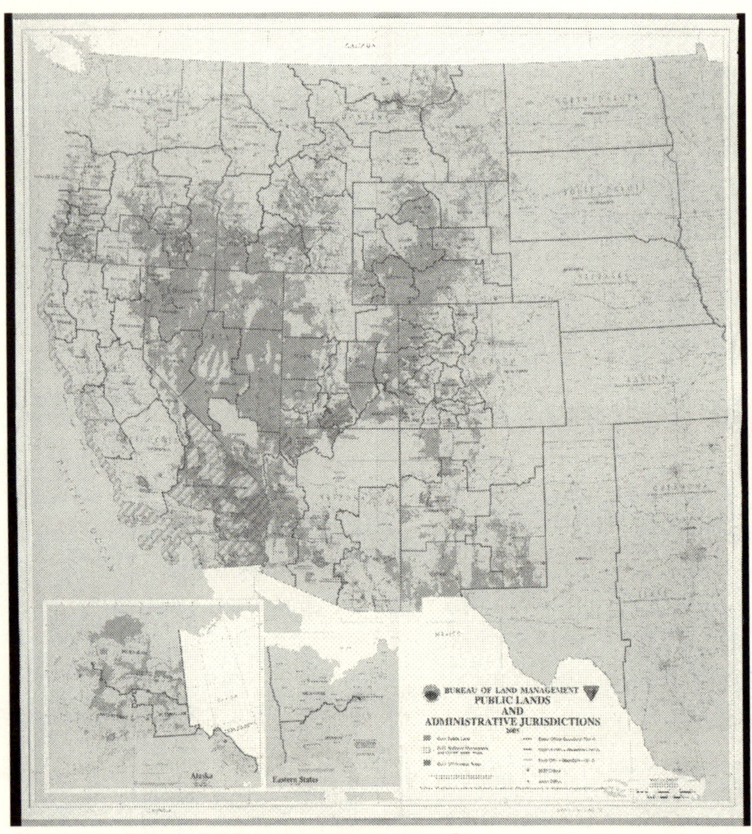

Bureau of Land Management Lands

National Monuments

Different federal agencies have responsibility for the nation's 128 national monuments, which occupy a middle ground between the tightly regulated national parks and the loosely regulated national forests and BLM lands. Grand Staircase-Escalante National Monument in southern Utah is a prime example. Managed by BLM, it contains some of the most picturesque scenery of the entire Colorado Plateau, yet many parts of it are open to dispersed camping.

National Preserves and National Recreation Areas

National preserves are run by the National Park Service and national recreation areas are run by differing federal agencies. They have less strict rules regarding resource extraction, so you may see evidence of logging, mining, or other commercial activities.

The good news is that they often also have less strict rules regarding recreation use: many of the larger ones do allow dispersed camping, although usually only in designated places or regions. (See "Our Story: Primo Spot in Mojave National Preserve" below.)

What About National Parks?

As a general rule, dispersed camping/boondocking is prohibited in national parks.

The great news about national parks? They are frequently surrounded by national forest or BLM land, especially in the West, which means you often have a wide variety of options for dispersed camping. For example, I have camped for free on national forest lands near Kings Canyon National Park, Yosemite National Park, Lassen Volcanic National Park, and Redwood National and State Parks in California, Crater Lake National Park in Oregon, Yellowstone National Park in Wyoming, Rocky Mountain National Park in Colorado, and

Canyonlands National Park, Capitol Reef National Park, Bryce Canyon National Park and Zion National Park in Utah, and Grand Canyon National Park in Arizona. Nearly all of these were excellent sites: private, flat, and frequently with stunning views, especially in the Colorado Plateau canyon country of Utah and Arizona.

Be aware that dispersed camping may be prohibited on federal lands near national parks to help combat over-crowding and harm to the environment, so you may have to drive a bit to find a spot.

Wildlife Management Areas (Federal and State)

Many wildlife management areas are quite extensive, and some allow dispersed camping, although many do not.

State Lands

Many states, especially in the West, have extensive holdings of public land in state forests and state wildlife management areas. Some state lands allow dispersed camping, but regulations vary from state to state, and often within a state. Some states also require purchase of a permit to use public lands.

Public Utilities

Some public utilities own large tracts of rural land. A few run organized campgrounds, like Pacific Gas and Electric in

California, and some may allow dispersed camping, or have remote campsites you can use for free.

Private Lands

Most of the forests not owned by the federal government or state governments are owned by private timber companies. Timber company land is often adjacent to or interspersed with Forest Service land, and Forest Service roads frequently cross timber company property and are the primary source of access, including for the removal of trees. Although there is some signage along forest roads indicating when you have crossed onto government land or onto private land, often it's not at all obvious.

Some timber companies actively encourage recreational use of their lands, particularly hiking, horseback riding, and hunting. Dispersed camping/boondocking is another matter, however. Companies may allow it for a very limited amount of time in a few locations, but they are very concerned about campfires turning into wildfires that burn their trees and their profits, and also about inconsiderate people leaving piles of trash.

Your best bet is to contact the national forest or other public land agency nearest the private land company and ask the name and contact info of the company, and if the public land agency happens to know the private company's rules about dispersed camping. If you find the actual name of the company, you can try searching their website and calling their main phone number.

I have camped on private lands in the past, always near national forests where I was usually researching trails for my hiking guidebooks, and never where it was obviously prohibited. I advise you to never camp on private timber lands if there are "No Trespassing" signs or any signs prohibiting camping, but I've always done it where no such signs were posted, and often it wasn't clear whether a given spot is on private land or public land. In my case, I typically show up in the early evening, eat, enjoy the scenery and the night sky, sleep in my vehicle, have an early breakfast, and then drive away to continue my research and explorations.

Canada: Our Neighbor to the North

This book is about dispersed camping in the United States; however, some of us want to explore the beautiful countries to the north and south.

A large majority of Canada is "Crown Land" that is available for public use, including dispersed camping and organized camping, plus opportunities to hike, mountain bike, kayak, etc. Access and dispersed camping are usually free for Canadian residents, but foreigners must buy a permit, and the costs can add up quickly.

Getting specific details of locations of Crown Lands, along with maps, allowed activities, and regulations, is not always easy. If you're traveling in Canada, search online using the name of the province and the term Crown Lands.

Mexico: Our Neighbor to the South

I love Mexico and speak quite a bit of Spanish. Stephanie and I spent three months traveling in the country, plus I've gone by myself for another three months. All of this was conventional travel using buses and planes and staying in apartments, hotels, and homes.

There are travelers who do dispersed camping in Mexico. It's overall a far riskier proposition in much of the country compared to the United States. Some regions have substantial gang activity, plus law enforcement is frequently not available or reliable.

If you are considering dispersed camping in Mexico, do thorough research first. Search online for "boondocking" and the specific state or states you want to visit. Facebook groups about Mexico travel can also be quite useful. In addition, check current State Department travel warnings.

Our Story: Primo Spot in Mojave National Preserve

Mojave National Preserve in Southern California features a jumbled array of rocky peaks interspersed with arroyos and plains, all covered with cacti, sagebrush, and extensive "forests" of Joshua trees. Stephanie and I visited near the height of a spring "super bloom," one of those rare occasions when abundant spring rains trigger ephemeral eruptions of wildflowers.

Camp for Free

We arrived at the Kelso Depot Information Center and approached the guy at the information desk. We first asked about the best hiking options along our planned route and established rapport. We then told him that we were traveling and sleeping in our van and were wondering about dispersed camping options, and at the same time we stressed that we practiced Leave No Trace principles.

Sunset at our primo dispersed campsite amidst the Joshua trees in Mojave National Preserve

We sensed a shift in his demeanor. He took his pen and marked a dirt road on our map, placing a few of red X's with official places for dispersed camping, and then said the road could be bit rough, but that we could make it in the Kia Sedona. He emphasized the importance of minimal impact, especially given the fragility of the desert environment. We sensed that he didn't share this information with everyone, that there were only a few such sites in Mojave National

Preserve, and that he only wanted the right people going there, people that would respect the land.

We headed down the dirt road and soon found a primo spot far from the main paved road with no one around. A nearby old and rough dirt road, blocked to traffic, led far back into the desert. We walked it multiple times, just the two of us, taking in the flowers, the crazy curved limbs of the Joshua trees, the many species of cacti, and the surrounding stark steepness of the mountains.

We had originally planned to stay just one night. However, this spot was so special we decided to stay a second night.

Lessons Learned

1. The importance of politeness and demonstrating respect for the land. We had the feeling that the guy working the information desk at the visitor center doesn't share those dispersed camping spots with just anybody. We asked politely and stressed that we were in a self-contained van and would behave ethically.

2. The importance of timing in your travels. We visited Mojave National Preserve in late spring when temperatures were still moderate (highs in the low 80s) and at the tail end of a rare super bloom.

3. The importance of flexibility. We loved our spot so much that we stayed an extra night so we could fully enjoy an area we'd never been to before and might never get back to again.

Chapter Four

Before You Go Dispersed Camping

In this chapter, we examine all the things you need to do before you actually drive into the backcountry to do dispersed camping, including researching the area or areas where you'll find your site or sites, plus deciding what to take and how to prepare your vehicle.

Note that there is some overlap here with "Chapter Five: Finding the Best Dispersed Camping Sites," primarily in researching sites, so make sure you look at that chapter also. You'll do most of this before you actually leave, but some of it you can do while you're on the road, like researching on your phone and especially stopping by a government agency office.

Where Do You Want to Go?

Big question! You have to figure out where you want to be, or where you might want to be. Think about what scenery/geography most appeals to you, typical weather characteristics (temperature, precipitation, winds) for the time of year, your favorite outdoor activities (hiking, mountain biking, fishing, nature observation), and, of course, your time frame.

Over the years, I've found that I prefer to drive less and spend more time getting to know a smaller territory in more detail. I develop a stronger sense of place by staying longer in a single area, and I also save substantial money on gas and wear and tear on my vehicle (plus I lower my carbon footprint).

What Is Your Time Frame?

This is important for determining how far (and how long) you're willing to drive. There's another important consideration involving time frame and itinerary. If you will be traveling a lot and usually finding a dispersed camping spot in the evening and then leaving in the morning, you'll have a lot more camping options because you can frequently camp at a level spot beside a secondary dirt road. However, if you want to stay put for two or more nights, you'll want a better spot that suits more of your needs, like shade, solitude, and accessibility to hiking trails and other features (see "Chapter 5: Finding the Best Dispersed Camping Sites").

Want More Solitude?

Some of us like to camp and explore away from others as much as possible. If that's you, here are four suggestions for finding more solitude in the wild.

First, go to less popular places. If you want to do dispersed camping around Moab, Utah or Yosemite National Park or Yellowstone National Park, you are going to have a lot of company. However, there are vast stretches of public lands that few people visit. While some are not as classically beautiful as others, many are.

Second, pick more remote camping spots. Most dispersed campers tend to cluster closer to attractions or small towns. Be willing to drive farther, and to head down roads that get less traffic.

Third, travel during shoulder seasons. This varies depending on where you want to go, but summer is usually prime time. If you can, travel in early May or in September, or even earlier or later.

Fourth, go midweek. Many people with jobs only have weekends available to be outside, but if you can get out there midweek, you'll have much more elbow room.

Get Official Recommendations and Check Regulations

This is crucial. For each national forest (including specific ranger districts/stations), BLM region, or other publicly owned land where you plan to camp, you need to be clear on where you can legally camp and any and all regulations regarding dispersed camping (see Chapter Three: Where You Can Go Dispersed Camping for typical regulations).

There are three ways to do this...

The first option and your best bet is to time your travel so you can drop by in person and visit the relevant ranger station or other agency office when it's open. That way you can pull out your map or maps (see below for more on maps) and get personalized recommendations based on the needs and desires of you and your party, and the capabilities of your vehicle. You can also learn about road closures or other restrictions, and you can also find out about official free campgrounds in remote areas that might interest you.

Don't have a map? You can usually buy one there, and if they happen to be out, they likely have one posted on a wall that you can take a picture of.

You can also obtain any needed permits. Although it's not common, some agencies require access permits (often for a fee). You may also need a permit to have a campfire, and the agency office can usually issue one, and let you know about any restrictions on campfires.

The second option: call. This can work reasonably well, especially if you have your maps in front of you and a specific list of questions. The person who answers the phone may not be the most knowledgeable about dispersed camping, so be sure to ask for the person who is.

Finally, you may be tempted to just check the agency's website and call it good. You will frequently find basic information there, but rarely will you get detailed specifics. Plus, agency websites are at times out of date. Most importantly, you won't get personalized attention and information.

Note: If you drive an RV, you especially want to make sure you know where you're going. You don't want to get stuck!

Get Unofficial Recommendations

Unofficial recommendations can be an excellent way to find good places to camp. Reach out to people you know who do dispersed camping and ask for their recommendations. Also strike up conversations with locals in the area and ask them.

There are also numerous online resources, including Facebook groups devoted to camping, traveling, hiking, and exploring specific geographic regions in the country. See dispersedcamping.net for a list of good websites and start searching on Facebook for suitable groups.

Two caveats regarding unofficial recommendations. First, you could get a recommendation for a spot where dispersed camping isn't actually allowed. Second, some people are unwilling to share their favorite spots, although they may be willing to direct you to other suitable areas.

Some Places Aren't Safe

There may also be areas that you think are suitable for dispersed camping but actually are not. Unfortunately, some public lands are sites of illegal activities, and the people involved in that don't want other people around. Another potential issue, especially near some towns, involves certain people out camping on public land who are heavy drug users that are more prone to have problems with neighbors (for more on this subject, see "Chapter Seven: Dispersed Camping Safety").

Agency personnel are a good source of information about safety concerns, and you can also glean useful info from websites and Facebook groups dedicated to dispersed camping, boondocking, and long-term living in vans, RVs and other vehicles.

Camping Prohibitions Near Towns

As popular towns with nearby public lands become even more popular, the agencies governing these areas frequently place restrictions on nearby dispersed camping, often prohibiting it entirely for a given distance from town.

Sedona, Arizona is one example. The last time I was there, I was driving a dirt road on Coconino National Forest and kept passing "Camping Prohibited" signs. I had to go quite a ways to find a legal place to camp.

Camping Prohibitions Near National Parks

Some national forests bordering national parks have been overwhelmed by dispersed campers who want to camp for free, or who can't find space in organized campgrounds. To combat overcrowding and degradation of natural areas, officials have instituted bans on dispersed camping in the vicinity of these national parks. Yosemite National Park in California is well-known example, but this situation exists around many major national parks in the West and in other parts of the country.

Get Good Maps

You need a good map or maps. Yes, often you can use your phone for maps (see below), but I always have one or more printed maps.

National forests and BLM regions all have maps for sale. The scale is usually quite large, meaning roads and other details are fairly small on the map, but these maps are invaluable for navigation, especially since they show road names and numbers you'll be seeing on signs, and they also indicate general conditions of roads (suitable for all vehicles or four-wheel-drive/high clearance only) and some road closures. In addition, they also show streams, lakes, mountains, hiking trails, and other geographic features.

Even more important are the motor vehicle use maps. You can often pick these up at the national forest office, and you can usually download them online as PDF files. These have similar road information as the larger maps, but they focus specifically on roads, are smaller scale, and more up to date.

Be aware that these maps can be out of date to varying degrees (check the year of publication). It could be, for example, that a road that was accessible to minivans when the map was printed now has deep and impassable gullies from a major rainstorm. Also, roads that show as open to drive may now be seasonally or permanently closed.

The US Geological Survey (USGS) has far-more-detailed maps (print and downloadable from their site) with a wealth of geographic information along with trails and roads, plus contour lines indicating elevations. Those contour lines are great for letting you know where you are most likely to find a level area to park your vehicle or pitch a tent.

You can also create and save/print custom USGS-based maps from websites. On Caltopo.com, for example, you can customize your map with Motor Vehicle Use Map and public lands data, plus other options, including GPS tracks for hiking trails (see dispersedcamping.net for more info.)

The major downside of USGS maps and maps derived from them is that many of the USGS maps are very old and they don't always accurately represent existing roads, especially their conditions and whether or not they are open. And if you plan on hiking, USGS maps can show trails that haven't been maintained for many years or even several decades and are thus difficult to follow.

This is why it's so important to call the government agency or, better yet, drop by in person, maps in hand. Agency personnel can give you all the details about road accessibility and conditions, plus current regulations and advice about exactly where to go, along with information about hiking trails and other recreational opportunities.

For example, I do much of my dispersed camping in the mountains of Northern California, the area I know best and the one I've written about extensively in my hiking guidebooks (see northerncaliforniahikingtrails.com). I always take national forest maps and motor vehicle use maps, and I also create and print specific topographic maps of the places I know I want to camp and hike.

Mount Shasta is the dominant landmark in upper Northern California.

Note: if you don't know how to interpret the contour lines on topographic maps, search for tutorials online. It's fairly easy once you get the hang of it.

Where to Obtain Maps

For printed national forest and BLM maps, the issuing agency is always a good source, and they may also have maps of adjacent forests/regions. REI and other outdoor stores usually have an excellent selection of printed maps. Call first to make sure the map you want is in stock. You can buy some maps on Amazon, but the selection is not comprehensive.

Google Maps

Google maps can also provide important information. Much public land is shaded green (although, unfortunately, not BLM lands, which are extensive in many desert areas of the United States). Don't count on it for exact boundaries, but it can be quite useful in some instances, especially if you already have GPS coordinates of a campsite.

Get Good Apps

There are multiple apps for your phone that provide detailed topographic maps with roads, trails, and natural features; some are specific for finding free campsites. See my website dispersedcamping.net for my current recommendations.

Download maps to your phone whenever possible so you don't have to be connected to cell service, which is often spotty or nonexistent in the wilds.

Careful! Don't count on your app or your phone! The app may stop working, your phone may stop working, your battery may drop to zero, or your phone could stop working. Always have printed maps as either a backup or as your primary source of navigation.

Google Earth

Google Earth provides detailed satellite images of the entire planet. It lets you zoom in on specific places to see the terrain, and also get specific GPS coordinates. It's especially useful for spotting dispersed camping sites in open terrain, but far less so in forests. You may even see vehicles at some spots, which often indicates it's a suitable dispersed camping site.

Be aware that Google Earth doesn't show what it looks like now. You'll see the date the image was taken.

Check the Weather

You'd think this is just common sense, but I meet people and read about others who went camping or hiking way in the boonies without checking the weather forecast. This can cause big problems!

My favorite weather source is the National Weather Service from NOAA (National Oceanic and Atmospheric Administration). You can use their website to get a point forecast for anywhere in the United States. I find the nearest town and then navigate the map to choose the point where I plan to be.

Be aware that weather can be drastically different over just a ten-mile distance. For example, during summer the high mountains may experience drenching thunderstorms, fierce winds, and cold temperatures, whereas a valley ten miles away and five thousand feet lower basks in sunshine and heat.

When checking the forecast for your travel dates, pay attention to all the relevant weather variables, including high and low temperatures, the probability of precipitation, wind speeds, and cloud cover.

One other piece of advice: read the forecast discussion. Here the meteorologist examines in detail what's going on, often including what different weather models say and what the likelihood is that the current prediction of weather 4-5 days from now could change, based on disagreement between models. Generally, the farther out the weather forecast, the lower the accuracy.

Of course, there are a variety of other websites and apps for weather data and forecasts. Most of these are fairly good, so if you have one you like and trust, keep using it. It never hurts to compare two or more sites.

Finally, a weather band radio is very useful for current forecasts. A few vehicle manufacturers include weather band radio as standard, and you can purchase in-dash radios with weather band, plus buy portable radios that include weather band, along with FM, AM, and even short-wave. Weather band radio is especially useful when you are out of cell phone range and can't access the Internet to get the latest forecast.

Careful! Don't rely on weather forecasts. Although they are usually reasonably accurate, sometimes they just aren't.

Always bring enough extra supplies so that you can wait out an unexpected spell of bad weather for a couple of days or more.

Make Sure Your Vehicle Is in Good Shape

Believe me, you don't want your vehicle to break down when you're in a tiny clearing at the far end of rough and narrow dirt road that's a long, long ways from a competent mechanic and is inaccessible or nearly so for a tow truck.

Check all your fluids and top off any that need it. If you patronize a business that specializes in oil and fluid changes, they may do this for free in-between services, or for a small fee. Or perhaps it's time to get your oil changed anyway, so you can get that done and have all your fluids checked and topped off. I say I'm going on a big trip and that I'd appreciate them looking for any potential problems.

Check all your tires for proper inflation and sufficient remaining tread. Also check that your battery functions properly. Your oil change place likely does this as part of the standard service.

You may also want to have your mechanic look over the vehicle, though this will likely entail a charge. If you're already having work done, mention that you'll be traveling in the backcountry and you want the entire vehicle checked for any potential problems.

Also bring at least some basics so you can get your vehicle running again yourself in certain situations:

-- Repair manual
-- Tool kit (even a basic one; you can purchase a kit from large department stores and online)
-- Spare tire (and perhaps even a second spare)
-- Tire inflator
-- Chains for snow and mud
-- A shovel (very helpful if you get stuck)
-- Car battery charger

You likely have a towing service, perhaps as part of your auto insurance or through an agency like the American Automobile Association (AAA). Frequently you can pay an extra fee that allows you to be towed a much longer distance at no extra charge.

Finally, top off your gas tank just before heading out into the back of beyond. If you'll be traveling extensively in truly remote places, like parts of Nevada, Utah, eastern Oregon, and other regions of the desert West, you may also need to carry extra gas in portable containers designed for that purpose.

Make Sure You Have a Good Towing Plan

A long tow can be very expensive. Consider paying extra now to get a plan that will tow you for free for the first hundred miles or more. You may be very glad someday!

Make Sure You Have Everything You Need

See "Appendix One: What to Take" for a detailed list of all the equipment and supplies you would likely want to take. You can also find the list on dispersedcamping.net, along with advice on where to buy everything at good prices.

Our Story: Waking Up to Snow

May is our favorite month to explore the desert sandstone country of southern Utah. Days are long and usually sunny, with moderate temperatures that are perfect for hiking. However, southern Utah in May can also see extremes of weather, including extended wet and cold periods.

And so it was for Stephanie and me in May of 2019. We were on our first trip in the new (to us) Kia Sedona. Our plan was to hit Zion National Park just for the day (it's now too crowded for our tastes), camp in the nearby forest overnight, and then explore Bryce Canyon National Park the next day.

Drenching rain soaked us on our hike in Zion National Park, and the weather forecast called for a 50% chance of precipitation overnight, with snow above 6,000 feet. We left Zion and headed north on Highway 89. I looked at the Dixie National Forest map and used it to select Utah 14, a paved road heading west toward Cedar City.

The road quickly climbed, and after a few miles we were on national forest land. I took the first likely looking dirt road on the right and we drove a mile until we found a level pull out beside the road. The temperature dropped quickly after dark and I was definitely concerned about snow.

Lucky I'm an early riser. I woke at the first light of dawn and looked out the window at a completely white landscape. I quickly dressed and went outside: three inches of snow with more falling at a heavy rate.

We had to get out of there! I quickly woke Stephanie and within five minutes I was behind the wheel, driving slowly and carefully through the snow, hoping for the best.

We made it back to paved Utah 14 without incident, and then we navigated carefully down through the snow to Highway 89, grateful to have escaped being snowbound high in the forest. The weather gradually improved and we were able to hike Bryce Canyon National Park that day, even with a bit of snow on the ground.

Last of the snow at Bryce Canyon National Park

Lessons Learned

1. Always check the weather report. We'd done that, and knew we'd be taking a chance of some snow.

2. If snow is forecast, determine the percentage probability; also find out the lowest predicted elevation and try hard to camp below it. I should have ascertained the elevation of the section of Dixie National Forest along Utah 14, which turned out to be quite high.

3. If it starts snowing, be ready to get out of there and drop down to lower elevations and/or safer paved roads that will be plowed.

4. If necessary, set an alarm for the middle of the night to check on snow levels, and be ready to move out then.

Chapter Five

Finding the Best
Dispersed Camping Sites

Alright, we're finally heading out to do dispersed camping! This chapter provides all the details you need to maximize the probability you'll find that perfect spot.

A perfect spot with a great mountain vista!

Make sure you've also read "Chapter Four: Before You Go Dispersed Camping." It includes important information about the initial research you'll do to determine where you'll be looking for dispersed camping sites.

So, you know the regulations for the general area you want to camp, you've gathered specific information from the governing agency, you have any required permits, plus you have maps, apps, and all your supplies. Let's get out there and find a primo dispersed camping site!

If you have specific directions to a specific place, of course you will follow those. The discussion here assumes you have either a fairly good idea of where you would like to camp (say within a mile or so), but don't know about a specific site, or that you're entering public land and are searching for a good spot while being far more open about its location.

Find Your Site in Daylight

I put this first because, as someone who has at times had to search for a site at night, I know from painful experience how much harder it is than searching in daylight. At night it's difficult to see side roads and road signs, and, when you do head down a side road looking for a site, it is very hard to actually see potential sites within the limited reach of your vehicle headlights.

Starting on a "Portal" Road

This is a main road on or quickly leading to BLM land, national forest land, or other public land where you plan to camp, and this is how you'll often enter public land. These roads almost always have room for two-way traffic and may even be paved, especially for the first few miles. The typical gravel or dirt surface is usually fairly good and is passable by regular cars, although there may be significant portions of washboard, plus a few moderate bumps, holes, and dips.

Careful! Be cautious on all roads after major rains or when snow is or could be present, including portal roads. Depending on the surface of the road, you can easily get stuck or slide off. Also be watching for oncoming traffic. Some roads are narrow and curvy, and you want plenty of time to stop if an SUV or a logging truck suddenly appears.

Portal roads are often not ideal for dispersed camping and frequently dispersed camping is prohibited along them, although this is not always the case. Just be aware that if you do find a legal dispersed camping site along a portal road, you'll likely have to deal with some traffic and its accompanying noise and dust, along with a lack of privacy and solitude.

Watch for "No Camping" Signs

As discussed in earlier chapters, many agencies have areas where dispersed camping is not allowed, usually near populated areas and campgrounds, and especially near popular areas that get many visitors, like national parks. And as just mentioned, you'll also frequently find that it's not allowed along main portal roads. Thus you'll see and should definitely obey those "No Camping" signs.

Watch for Secondary Roads

This is the key to finding your spot!

Secondary roads leave from portal roads. They may run for several miles or more, or they can be quite short. The condition can vary from suitable for passenger cars to high-clearance only.

How to Pick a Good Secondary Road: Road Characteristics

Most importantly, it must be suitable for your vehicle. Of course, you can't always tell from initial appearances. However, find the road on your agency map or other mapping tools and then check the map legend. Roads are often designated by vehicle suitability. As discussed in "Chapter Four: Before You Go Dispersed Camping," this can change over time and, if anything, road conditions are more likely to get worse than better, since agencies typically have only limited funds for road maintenance.

Once you've checked the map (when feasible) you want to check four important characteristics of the road.

First, are the surface characteristics suitable for your vehicle? This is a function primarily of clearance but also the surface itself (gravel, dirt, rocks, mud, water). Will you possibly need all-wheel drive/four-wheel-drive, and/or high clearance? Any chance you could get stuck?

Second, is the road wide enough? In some areas, brush and/or trees can intrude on the road and potentially scratch your vehicle. Only you can decide how much you're willing to risk getting your ride scratched, and depending on the characteristics of the vegetation, many scratches may be superficial and disappear after a good washing. On the other hand, a thick branch could leave a permanent major scratch.

Third, what's the likelihood you can turn around if you have to? This can be hard to predict accurately, but look for level areas farther along the probable route of the road. Also check the road at the beginning: do you see places to turn around? If so, it's a good indication that there may be other such areas farther along. (If you have to actually back out a dirt road, have a companion get behind you so you can be guided via mirrors, and if you are backing downhill, tilt your outside mirrors down a bit to make it easier to see the road itself).

Fourth, how much use does the road get? Look at the number of tire tracks and try to assess how fresh they are; you can often infer information about the size and nature of the vehicles that have travelled the road by examining the distance between tires and the width of the tires themselves. Lots of fresh tracks means the road is accessible to at least some vehicles, hopefully vehicles like yours, but it can also mean other people are down there who have already snagged the best camping sites. No or minimal tracks could mean the road is difficult to travel, or it could mean you'll find a secluded spot with no neighbors.

"When in doubt, scout." If a road looks like it might be too rough, or narrow, or in any way unsuitable for your vehicle, or if it's on the edge of being unsuitable, and you're either worried about it getting even worse, or you think a good camping spot could be just around the bend—get out of the vehicle and walk the road until you get your answer.

This includes checking the depth of streams you need to cross and also large puddles in the road.

Be careful you don't get your vehicle stuck! See "Chapter Seven: Dispersed Camping Safety" for advice on both how not to get stuck in the first place, and also to get unstuck, if necessary.

And a final consideration: do you have an older vehicle or a vehicle more prone to break down? If so, consider picking roads that a tow truck or at least a mobile mechanic can negotiate easily, and also strongly consider buying a tow plan that will tow you long distances for no extra charge.

Stopping to scout the possibilities

How to Pick a Good Secondary Road: Where Does It Go?

A good secondary road should look like it will lead to a place where you can camp. Most importantly, do you think you are likely to find a level area suitable for dispersed camping? Even relatively steep terrain may have level areas, especially if it has been logged in the past and has level spots bull-dozed for loading logging trucks. Use your maps, especially topographic maps, in combination with your eyeballs to help you pick your secondary road.

A good secondary road should also look like it will lead into territory that you find attractive, primarily in terms of natural features. Is it forested? Does it lead to lakes or streams? Might you be able to find a site with vistas? Are there hiking trails nearby?

Important: How to Not Get Lost on Secondary Roads!

Once you leave a main portal road, you may potentially wind up driving quite a ways. If you aren't careful, you can make two or three turns onto other roads and then not remember how to get back to the portal road.

When you first turn onto a secondary road, use a system to record what roads you take, which turns you make onto other roads, and how far you go on each road. Either dictate into your phone or a digital recorder, or have a companion write down the relevant information. Also consider marking your progress on the physical map. Don't trust your memory! If it fails, you can spend a lot of time trying to find your way out. I know this from experience!

Just at the entrance to the secondary road, do the following.

If you have a mapping app on your phone and you know how to use it correctly, definitely start GPS tracking at the entrance of the secondary road.

Note the name of the road. Most roads (but not all) have some sort of name. For example, national forest roads usually have a combination of numbers and letters.

Reset your trip odometer to zero so that distances are easier to measure. Most vehicles have a button for this near the vehicle mileage and the speedometer.

Each time you take another road, note the road name and the trip odometer reading, and whether you turned left or right.

Once you find your camping spot, be sure to note the final trip odometer reading and also save your GPS track, if you used a tracking app.

One final piece of advice: if you come to a junction without any signage, take a picture of it with your phone that you can refer to later, if necessary.

Choosing Your Dispersed Camping Site

When feasible, I seek sites along a secondary road off of a secondary road. This typically gives the best combination of accessibility, privacy, and beauty.

Here's what to look for in a dispersed camping site.

Finding the Best Dispersed Camping Sites

Always use an existing site whenever possible. You'll see obvious places where people have parked vehicles and often there will be a fire ring. (Note: never drive off-road or over vegetation to find a place for dispersed camping. This disrupts the environment and is always against agency rules. For more, see "Chapter Six: Dispersed Camping Best Practices.")

Is the site safe? Is it located in or near a wash that could fill with water in a flash flood? Is it right below a cliff? Could large branches fall off a tree, or is there a tree leaning over the site that could fall?

Is the site level, or level enough? If you sleep in your vehicle, can you park it in such a way that you'll be able to sleep comfortably? If you pitch a tent, is there a suitable spot? If you can't sleep level, arrange your vehicle or tent such that your head is pointed uphill and that there's no or only minimal sloping left or right. (Safety note: Always engage your parking brake; you don't want your vehicle to roll, especially in the direction of a tent.)

Make sure there's enough room for your vehicle and anything else you plan to use, such as a tent, a portable table, or chairs. Also keep in mind that if the site is large and located in a popular area, you may have others who want to share it with you (see below).

Look for a site with your desired level of privacy. I personally prefer to be out of sight of other people as much as possible.

Think about the nearness of water. You may want the water for drinking (after filtering or other treatment), for washing, and perhaps also to swim in. Also keep in mind that nearby water, especially lakes and ponds, often means lots of mosquitoes in summer. Agency regulations always require you to be a certain distance from water, usually at least 100 feet and often 200 feet.

A key consideration is the nearness of the site to any recreation activities you want to do. I love to hike, so being able to walk on dirt roads, nearby trails, or even cross-county is important to me.

Think about where you want to situate your vehicle or tent in terms of sun exposure. The sun rises in the east and sets in the west, with a much higher trajectory in summer and a lower, more southerly, one in winter. If it's hot, shade will be a major factor, so plan accordingly. Conversely, if it's cold, you likely want your vehicle in full sun during the day.

You may also want to consider the moon, especially if you sleep in your vehicle with uncovered windows near your face. I've had some difficulty sleeping a few times when the full or near-full moon was shining directly on my face through the windows of my vehicle. Check online for the current phase and rising and setting times of the moon.

If phone reception is important, you'll want a site closer to cell towers and with more open terrain.

An excellent spot: level, no hazards, lots of privacy, and beautiful scenery!

Found Your Site? Check a Little Farther...

When you find a good site, park your vehicle to establish occupancy, and then walk a little ways farther down the road. You may find an even better site, or you might see something that makes you not want to stay at the site you selected, like someone else camping nearby, or evidence of current logging. In addition, you'll learn more about the lay of the land, including natural features and places to walk and explore.

Sharing a Site with Strangers?

I always prefer to not share a site. If you come upon a site that's occupied, you should just keep driving to find your own site. If you are truly desperate, like it's near dark or you are concerned you won't be able to find another level place anywhere, you can strike up a conversation with the people already there and ask if they are willing to share the site.

If you do this, think about it from their perspective. Of course, they want privacy, which they'll lose with you there, but they may be open to it as long as they feel you are both safe and will be a good neighbor. It can help to say you'll be moving on the next morning.

What if the situation is reversed and someone wants to share your site? You have three options: politely refuse, agree to share the site, or give them the site and go find another one. The specific circumstances will dictate your response. (More details in "Our Story" below).

Dispersed Camping and Boondocking with Others

While many of us prefer to find isolated spots, some people also like to gather together in specific sites to socialize and share information and tips.

The best-known of these is the winter gathering on BLM land near Quartzsite, Arizona. You have to pay a fee, but, at the time of this writing, you can stay the entire winter if you like. The Quartzsite gathering is especially popular with RV folks who like boondocking. Other areas are also popular for informal gatherings. Search the Internet and pay attention to RV/boondocking/van nomad groups on Facebook.

Keep a List of Your Favorite Spots

The more you do dispersed camping, the more great spots you'll find, spots you want to come back to again.

Don't assume you'll remember how to find them! Do what I do: create a folder on your computer for all related files, like PDFs of topographic maps (which you can annotate with most PDF programs) and Word documents with important details, including GPS coordinates. You can also save any audio notes or relevant pictures. In addition, I have a set of physical folders by geographic region where I put print maps and related materials.

Stephanie's Story: "Just a Little Farther…"

We have travelled down many a dirt road to find a great campsite. Sometimes we find the perfect spot within a few minutes, other times it seems to take 30 minutes. When we reach the 10-minute mark, I often lose hope and suggest we turn back and try another road. John, optimistically, will say, "Let's go a little farther." Much to my surprise, John is right about 95% of the time and we do find the perfect dispersed camping site.

Lessons Learned

1. Advance research and experience are important in finding dispersed camping sites. We (usually) do substantial research before we go looking for a spot, plus we get better

and better at reading terrain and the nature of dirt roads, and assessing the most likely places to find a spot.

2. It's also important to listen to your intuition!

Our Story: Someone Wants to Share the Site

Several years ago in Grand Staircase-Escalante National Monument, Stephanie and I had found our best site ever at the end of a small dirt road. It sat on the edge of a steep drop with a full view of the Escalante River drainage and 20 miles beyond to the high mountains of the Aquarius Plateau: all sandstone in colors ranging from cream to ochre to orange to salmon to deep red.

The view from our campsite

Finding the Best Dispersed Camping Sites

Back then we traveled in the Subaru Outback and slept in a tent. All was perfect: the weather, the beauty, being with each other. We set up the tent, ate dinner, and settled back to watch the colors shift as the sun neared the horizon.

And then a vehicle drives up and stops 150 feet away. "They'll turn around," I said.

But they don't. After a few moments they pull forward and park right next to us. Two women get out.

"We're camping here, too," said one of the women in an authoritative voice.

"There's plenty of other places to camp farther down the main road," I said in a diplomatic tone.

"We want to stay here. It's beautiful and we've been driving all day." And with that they started unpacking.

Stephanie and I begrudgingly accepted the inevitable. We couldn't make them leave. We could leave ourselves, but this was the best spot ever, and it was early evening and we'd already set up camp.

We were even more disappointed five minutes later when they put up their tent right next to ours, like just five feet away. Now, this was the optimal place to set up a tent, being both level and right on the edge with the killer view, but there were other level spots without the view.

"This the best spot, so we're putting our tent here."

Camp for Free

We decided we didn't want the situation to be any more uncomfortable than it was, so we introduced ourselves and made a bit of small talk so it would be an overall friendly situation.

And so we slept right next to them that night. They were quiet and respectful once they'd established themselves. But still, we'd much, much rather they weren't there!

More recently I was alone in the Kia Sedona at a large site near a stream bordering the Trinity Alps Wilderness on the Klamath National Forest in Northern California. I was mixing work on a freelance writing project with hiking nearby trails.

Late one morning, two vehicles show up, an SUV and a large RV. They stop on the dirt road just before the turnoff to the site. A man gets out and walks up to me, obviously disappointed that I'm there. I greet him politely and he quickly asks If I'm camping there. I tell him yes, but that I'm only planning on staying another night or two.

He then says that he has a mining claim nearby on the stream and that this is where he and his wife park every year for three months, from mid-summer into fall, and that they really, really need to set up right here, even if they have to share the site with me. And he didn't sound happy about it. His wife had joined us. She never said a word; she just looked at me through her mirror sunglasses while smoking a cigarette.

That settled it for me. I offered the entire site to them, packed up my stuff, and drove a half-mile farther along to another site. It wasn't as nice as the one I'd left, but it had a level spot to park and, most of all, privacy.

Lessons Learned

1. Things don't always go your way. Sometimes you have to adjust to changing circumstances.

2. Be willing to leave and find another place if you either don't like the situation or it's truly better for the other people to let them have the site.

Boondocking Notebook/Journal

I've created a journal that lets you record all the key data about each dispersed camping site, including the details of how you got there and what you most enjoyed.

You'll find it on Amazon by searching for the exact title, or title keywords along with "John Soares" (and click the cover to "Look Inside.")

Chapter Six

Dispersed Camping Best Practices

This chapter details the important ways you should minimize your impact on the environment when you're dispersed camping. These practices promote the long-term health of the planet, and they make it less likely that government agencies will restrict access to the backcountry.

A level and safe existing site in Grand Staircase-Escalante National Monument

Camp and Walk on Durable Surfaces

When driving your vehicle and choosing and setting up your campsite, make sure you stay on durable surfaces that can best withstand the impact of your passing. Stay out of moist areas like meadows and well away from sensitive soils, like the cryptogamic soils that are common in the Southwest.

When walking around your campsite or exploring on foot, stay on established trails whenever possible. When not possible, try to step on rocks and other durable surfaces such that you minimize the disturbance of your passing.

Pack It Out, All of It

Make sure you remove all of your garbage, including organic waste such as apple cores, banana peels, and orange rinds.

And go a step beyond and remove any other trash you find. We always take an extra garbage bag, which has come in handy a few times when we came upon campsites previously inhabited by thoughtless people.

Campfires: Skip Them!

I strongly urge you to forego campfires. Here are nine good reasons why:

1. Campfires don't work anywhere near as well as a portable stove (or the stove in your vehicle) for cooking food. They heat unevenly, it's difficult to get the correct temperature,

they cover your cooking pots with greasy soot, and all too often ash winds up in your food.

2. Unless you brought firewood from home (which is often prohibited so you don't bring in invasive pests), you'll be using wood from near your campsite. Doing so removes that wood from the local ecosystem, where its slow decay is an important part of replenishing soil nutrients. (Although in some fire-prone forests in the West, using downed wood is encouraged to help reduce the fuel load on the forest floor.)

3. Campfires overall don't provide much warmth, unless they are big. Bring plenty of warm clothes suitable for nighttime temperatures and you'll be fine.

4. Campfires emit lots of smoke, which means the wind will at least occasionally blow it on you, stinging your eyes and making your clothes smell. In addition, breathing in smoke is not good for your lungs and overall health.

5. Campfires are bright, depriving you of the ability to see the stars. When necessary, use a portable lantern for illumination.

6. Campfires can be visible for miles, which is not good if you prefer that others not know about you and your dispersed camping spot.

7. Campfires take time to start, maintain, and put out, plus the time needed to gather firewood, time you could spend doing something else more fun.

8. You need to douse a campfire thoroughly with water, which means either getting said water from a stream or lake, or using the limited amount of water you brought with you.

9. Finally, your campfire could spark a wildfire, with all the danger and damage that wildfires entail. In many states you are liable for the costs of suppressing a wildfire you start, plus you can be sued for damages.

Stephanie and I almost never have a campfire. We stay outside in the dark as long as we want talking and looking at the stars, and then we read in the front of the van until we're ready to sleep.

Trash left by previous visitors at this dispersed campsite. We packed out their trash, and we didn't have a fire.

Campfires: If You Must

I get that some of you like campfires. And I do have good memories of hanging around the fire with my companions back when I did a lot of backpacking.

Here are the eleven key considerations for safely and ethically having a campfire:

1. Make sure campfires are allowed. Many states, especially in the forested West, impose bans by midsummer on all campfires outside of developed, official campgrounds (the ones with picnic tables and numbered sites). Climate change has led to increased frequency of years with low snowpack and precipitation, along with overall hotter temperatures, prime conditions for the start and spread of wildfires. These bans are always published online, and there are typically signs posted along roads leading to the backcountry.

2. Make sure you have a permit, if required. California requires a campfire permit for all campfires outside of developed campgrounds, and other states may follow suit in the future. You can get the permit either online or at many national forest and BLM offices, and at other California agencies.

3. Always use an existing campfire ring, when available. You'll find most dispersed camping sites already have a user-created campfire ring, so use it.

4. If you absolutely must create a new campfire ring, do this:

Dispersed Camping Best Practices

-- Choose a level spot with no or minimal combustible plant materials, like downed wood and dry grass.

-- Use a shovel or other implement to clear an area 10 feet or so in diameter.

-- Create a small depression in the soil in the center of the area where you want the actual fire.

-- Place a ring of rocks around the depression at least six inches high.

5. Use dead and downed wood, especially the smaller pieces. Never remove wood from trees or shrubs, even if it appears dead.

6. Only burn as much wood as you need. Plan accordingly so that when you're ready to sleep, the fire has burned down to coals.

7. Don't burn trash. This releases harmful chemicals into the atmosphere, and often leaves nonflammable residual material in the bed of the campfire.

8. Don't leave the fire unattended. You are responsible for having a safe fire. You or a companion must be near the fire and watching it all times so you can quickly respond if the fire escapes the fire ring.

9. Think about preventing the spread of the fire. A key factor here is wind. Strong winds can pick up sparks from the fire and blow them far beyond the cleared space for the fire ring, potentially causing a wildfire. If it's really windy, forego the campfire.

10. Have plenty of water nearby, a shovel for quickly putting dirt on flames, and a multipurpose fire extinguisher.

11. Ensure the campfire is completely out. Use plenty of water and perhaps dirt from around the campfire ring. The fire should be cold to the touch, emitting no heat at all.

Pooping and Peeing

Many of you have toilets inside your vehicles (or portable toilets), so you're basically covered (but see below if you also pee outside).

Everybody poops. If you need to do it outside in a remote area, find a spot at least 200 feet from water and far from trails and campsites. The ideal spot is forest duff where you can easily dig a hole six to ten inches deep to do your business. When you're done, refill the hole and tamp it down a bit with your foot. There are special little shovels you can buy, or you can just bring a garden trowel from home. If you have neither, use a stout stick or the heel of your boot.

Pack out your toilet paper! I'm serious. Initially it's a little gross, but you'll quickly get used to it. I use a large zip lock bag that I then put inside another plastic bag.

You'll also need to pack out your poop in popular areas and in the desert. As more people use the backcountry, the ever-growing amount of poop out there is becoming a serious problem. Packing it out is especially important in desert environments where it's difficult to dig holes and the soil cannot break down poop quickly. There are several ways to pack it out, including commercially available bagging systems, but you can also do it yourself with a combination of zip-lock bags and other plastic bags.

Everybody pees. When peeing outside, do it far away from water sources and try to spread it around on the ground so it's not concentrated on a single plant. Women, pack out your toilet paper.

Staying Clean

If you have a shower in your vehicle, lucky you! For everyone else, you can use a portable shower or even jugs of water. Use biodegradable soaps and wash yourself far from streams and lakes. Of course, a good swim also helps keep you clean.

Washing Dishes Outside

Follow the same advice for outdoor showers: be sure to use biodegradable soaps and do it far from streams and lakes, and also your campsite. Do the best you can to minimize food particles on the ground that can attract bears and other animals.

Respect Wildlife

Give wildlife plenty of space to go about their daily lives without having to alter their behavior due to your presence.

Use the "rule of thumb": extend your arm and hold out your thumb. If your thumb completely covers the critter, you are likely far enough away. If it doesn't, you are likely too close.

If you take your dog, consider limiting its ability to roam freely, at least part of the time. Dogs scare away a lot of wildlife and also disturb their feeding patterns and other behaviors.

Respect Plants and Rocks

Minimize your disturbance of the environment by leaving plants and rocks in place. This doesn't mean you can't take home a beautiful rock, but make sure it's allowed. Some jurisdictions prohibit removing any materials.

Be a Good Neighbor

If other people are around, do what you reasonably can to allow them to have a good camping experience.

Start by giving them space and privacy. If you come to a larger dispersed camping area that has room for multiple parties, select a spot that's as far from others as reasonably possible while still meeting your needs.

Also be relatively quiet. This is not the place for playing music through speakers. If you want to listen to music, use ear buds. And be respectful of others' sleeping. Do your best to keep all noise down between 10 p.m. and 8 a.m.

In addition, consider light pollution. Your campfire or outside lantern can mean that nearby campers don't get to enjoy a dark sky. It's polite to ask neighbors if they mind your fire or lantern, or if there is a compromise you can reach about how much light you'll be producing, and when.

Finally, be open to meeting new people. We've met many fascinating folks in the backcountry over the years, some of whom are now our friends.

My Story: Dark Skies and Starry Nights

The night sky has fascinated me ever since I was a little boy. As I grew older, my fascination blossomed into a love of astronomy, which was actually my first major in college.

I was fortunate to grow up in the countryside outside of Anderson in far Northern California, where dark skies were common, but it was on my first backpacking trips in the nearby Trinity Alps as a teenager when I first saw truly dark and clear skies.

I soon learned all the constellations and the brightest stars, and eventually I explored more deeply with binoculars and telescopes, looking at galaxies, star clusters, and nebulae.

I still really enjoy a truly dark sky filled with stars, and dispersed camping is the best way to make it happen.

Does staring up at a dark night sky appeal to you? If so, here's how to maximize your enjoyment:

1. Check the weather. Cloudy sky = no stars! However, partly cloudy skies may have brilliantly clear patches that allow good observing.

2. Check the phase of the moon (easy to do online, and also visually). Anything more than a sliver (2-3 days old) will wash out the fainter stars in the sky, so try to plan your trip accordingly. It's still great to look at the sky with a moon, and to look at the moon itself, but if you're like me, it's the truly dark skies you want.

3. Also find out which planets are visible, and when. In addition, research meteor showers, including the best days and times to view them, and the expected number of meteors per hour.

4. Pick a region at high elevation. All other things equal, the higher the elevation, the better the seeing.

5. Choose a camping spot either in or just beside a clearing. You want a substantial portion of the sky open, so avoid the forest.

6. Take binoculars. Any binoculars will do, but more expensive binoculars with wider lenses will show you more stars and other celestial objects, and it will all be brighter and clearer.

7. Find the Milky Way and sweep along it. This is where you'll see the coolest stuff.

8. Consider taking printed star charts or a star atlas. This will let you learn the constellations and major celestial objects.

9. Buy a red flashlight for use with the atlas in the dark. The red light will preserve your night vision.

10. Yes, there are apps for identifying everything in the night sky. Point your phone and the app will tell you exactly what you're looking at. Note that the light of your phone will reduce your night vision, and that's why I prefer the old-fashioned method of star charts with a red flashlight.

The high desert of northeastern California is perfect for watching the stars: high elevation and open sky.

Chapter Seven

Dispersed Camping Safety

Dispersed camping is overall a very safe activity, as long as you prepare properly, have the right knowledge, take the right equipment and supplies, and make the right decisions. In this chapter I provide information on a wide variety of topics related to your safety, so pay close attention and take the advice to heart.

Note: some of the information here is also covered in other parts of the book, especially "Chapter Five: Finding the Best Dispersed Camping Sites." It's repeated or at least referenced here to make sure you don't miss it.

Pick a Safe Area

You're unlikely to have problems with theft or other crime in most parts of the backcountry. That said, there are some areas, especially closer to towns and in a few regions where illegal marijuana grows are common, where you are more likely to have issues.

Ask the governing agency about the safety situation either in person or over the phone; the local police are also a good source of intel. Conversations with locals can also be helpful, and you may also find information online.

To minimize the chance someone will see my camping spot, I typically look for a place that's off major dirt roads, preferably well out of sight. "Chapter Five: Finding the Best Dispersed Camping Sites" has all the details.

Check the Weather

This is very important! You don't want to get snowed in way back in the mountains, and if rain, thunderstorms, or strong winds are in the forecast, you need to take that into account when picking your campsite (see below). I recommend the National Weather Service. (See "Chapter Four: Before You Go Dispersed Camping.")

Don't Get Lost When Searching for Campsites

"Chapter Five: Finding the Best Dispersed Camping Sites" provides thorough coverage of this topic. Make sure you have good maps and apps (and know how to use them), and that you pay close attention to the different turns you make on roads, especially once you leave the main road. Also see below for advice on not getting lost when exploring.

Watch Out for Other Vehicles

You'll be sharing the roads with other vehicles, some of them traveling in the opposite direction. Backroads can be curvy and narrow, and a few people drive too fast.

Be especially wary in areas of active logging. Sometimes these areas are signed, and you may also see signs on trees advising loggers which channels to use on their radios to communicate with each other. Logging truck drivers generally drive safely, but they may not be expecting you.

Watch Out for Animals

Lots of critters, large and small, wander near and on roads. I've nearly hit bears, deer, and cows, not to mention racoons, skunks, squirrels, and chipmunks. Be especially careful near dusk and after dark when deer are active, and remember: if you see one deer crossing the road, there's a good chance one or more others are getting ready to do the same thing. If you're traveling in cattle country, slow way down if you see bovines near the road and be careful not to spook them, which can cause them to stampede into fences and get hurt.

Don't Get Stuck

Proper planning will help you avoid most situations where you could potentially get stuck. Talk to agency personnel about the conditions of the roads you plan to drive, including the presence of snow. Also assess recent weather. Have significant storms likely made dirt roads muddy and left large puddles of water? And what about coming weather? Any storms in the forecast?

Bring proper tools and materials: a shovel, sand or cat litter (not the clay type) for traction, and other items that you can lay on the ground in an emergency.

You're most likely to get stuck in mud, deep sand, deep dirt, or snow. Remember the advice from "Chapter Five: Finding the Best Dispersed Camping Sites": **when in doubt, scout**. If a stretch of road looks sketchy, stop your vehicle and get out and investigate. How deep is the potential hazard? (Use a stick or shovel.) Can you safely drive around it? Can you drive with the wheels on one side on a good surface for traction? Remember: better safe than sorry. If you have any concerns you might get stuck, turn around and go find someplace else to camp.

If you're driving and suddenly find yourself in bad situation with a strong possibility of getting stuck, the most important thing to do is keep going in the direction of safer ground. Moderate the throttle and don't accelerate too quickly, which can increase the likelihood of getting stuck; play with throttle to find the sweet spot where you get the best traction and safe forward movement. It may help to move the steering wheel slightly from side to side. Do not drive through previous vehicle tracks; the mud or dirt in the tracks will be softer and more difficult to navigate.

But If You Get Stuck, Do This

Once you can no longer move forward, take your foot off the gas. Don't keep spinning the wheels, which will just cause you to sink deeper and make the situation worse.

The key point is to get traction to the drive wheels, the ones to which your engine provides power. You can use sand or kitty litter, as mentioned above. You can also use materials you have in your vehicle, like a tarp, a yoga mat, even the floor mats (while recognizing that these items will likely sustain significant damage). Also look to your immediate surroundings. There may be gravel, sand, small sticks, downed branches, leaves, or other materials that you can put under the drive wheels to provide traction.

You may be able to use your shovel or another improvised implement to dig around your tires and to clear a path forward for your vehicle.

You can also try deflating your tires a bit, which will give improved traction. Let out five PSI at a time, and not more than 15 PSI. Be sure to inflate your tires back to the recommended pressure as soon as possible.

If your vehicle can move slightly forward and backward, try the rocking method. Put it in reverse and then quickly into forward gear, repeating quickly to get a rocking motion that can build enough momentum to get you moving forward. Note that this can be hard on your engine and transmission, so don't overdo it.

If other people are around, have them push on the vehicle as you try to move forward.

It's also possible to attach your vehicle to another with a tow strap or winch cable and use that vehicle to give yours enough momentum to drive out on your own. Make sure you know how to safely connect the two vehicles so that you cause no damage, and that you carefully coordinate the maneuver so that the two vehicles move slowly and match speeds until the stuck vehicle reaches safe ground.

If you can't remove the vehicle yourself, you'll have to call a tow truck.

Choosing Your Site: Avoid Natural Hazards

Pay attention to potential natural hazards when you're evaluating a potential campsite.

1. Is the site in an area that can flood in a major rainstorm or thunderstorm? This is most relevant in desert areas of the Southwest, where it may not be immediately obvious to the casual observer that a spot is actually in or near a dry wash. Major thunderstorms are common in summer in the desert, and they can lead to flash floods.

2. Cliffs and steep slopes are another hazard. Rocks can fall down on you, your vehicle, or equipment, or the slope itself could slide down on you.

3. Also look at trees. Do any of them look like they are ready to fall on your campsite? What about major branches?

4. Is the site relatively safe from lightning strikes, especially if thunderstorms are in the forecast? Avoid wide open areas where you and your vehicle are the tallest objects (and see below for more on lightning safety).

Don't Count on Cell Phone Coverage

Don't assume you'll be able to reach 911 or other sources of help if there's a problem. Yes, you may have cell coverage where you camp, but often there's no coverage, especially in remote areas. In addition, your cell phone could stop working or the battery could drop to zero.

Definitely consider a satellite phone or SPOT device, especially if you spend a lot of time out in the backcountry. It's a fairly expensive proposition, so thoroughly research current devices and plans.

Two-way radios (walkie talkies) can allow good communication between you and members of your party, particularly over relatively short distances, but geographic features, especially mountains, can block the signal.

A safe dispersed camping site in Northern California

Water

Water is crucial for staying alive. Always bring substantially more than you need—I usually do 50-100% more—and make sure you factor in all the ways you'll use water, including drinking, washing dishes, washing your hands and body, brushing your teeth, and putting out the campfire at night.

If you're still in civilization and don't have enough water, you can usually find it for free at parks, picnic areas, visitor centers, and town drinking fountains. You may even be able to fill up at a pay campground.

In addition to bringing your own water, also have one or more ways to treat water from streams and lakes. Filters are the best option, but there are also chemical methods. Pay attention to your surroundings so you know the location of the nearest water and know how to reach it.

Sanitation

At a minimum, keep your hands relatively clean by washing them with water and biodegradable soap, or by using antiseptic gel, especially after pooping.

First Aid

Take a good first aid kit. These are widely available at outdoor stores, large department stores, and online. Thoroughly investigate what's in your kit, and then supplement it with anything else you think you might need.

Also bring a book on first aid. Bonus points if you actually take a first aid class; these are offered regularly in most towns and cities.

Medications

You'll have pain relievers in your first aid kit, but also make sure that you and every member of your party has all the medications they take regularly, or even occasionally. Also bring several days' more than you need, just in case you wind up spending more time in the backcountry than you expected.

Manage Your Power

This is a potentially complicated subject that's well beyond the scope of this book, but the key point is to make sure you don't drain your vehicle battery so much that you can't start your rig. Be careful with how much you use lights, listen to music, and also run appliances through the 12-volt plugs. Consider purchasing a voltmeter and learning how to use it.

It's a good idea to have a fully charged portable battery charger, just in case.

Campfires

If you have a campfire, be very careful that you follow proper practices to prevent its spread. I go into this in great detail in "Chapter Six: Dispersed Camping Best Practices," so head there for more specifics.

Wildfires

Wildfires are a significant hazard, especially in the West from early summer well into fall. Here's what to do to minimize your chances of having to deal with one.

1. Before you go, check for any existing wildfires near your planned location, including any warnings prohibiting travel and also predictions for fire growth and containment. State and federal fire-fighting agencies have websites and issue frequent updates; they also often provide updates on social media.

2. Before you go, check the weather forecast. Especially look for red-flag warnings and the predicted probability and location of thunderstorms (and their associated lightning). Also check the weather forecast periodically while you're out camping.

3. Plan your escape route(s). As you peruse maps and find your dispersed camping site, think about different ways you can get away if a wildfire approaches. It's best to have at least two possible routes going in two different directions.

4. If you see smoke, observe its distance, direction of movement, and quantity, along with wind speeds. This helps you assess the potential danger. If you can, access the Internet to see what information you can find about the fire's potential danger to you.

5. It's always better to be safe than sorry. If you feel there is any significant danger, get out of there.

Lightning

Thunderstorms and lightning can occur during any season, though they are most common in summer and at higher elevations, especially in the late afternoon and early evening. A point-forecast weather report for your specific location will give you the probability and potential severity of thunderstorms.

If thunderstorms and lightning are a possibility, choose a campsite that's away from open areas and near trees. You are actually fairly safe inside your vehicle in a thunderstorm, but don't touch any metal surfaces.

If you are out hiking and see tall thunderheads, get away from exposed ridges and peaks and head for the shortest trees in the nearest forest. If lightning strikes nearby, keep a good distance from any hiking companions, let go of any trekking poles, and squat on your daypack.

Hunters

The odds are very, very low that a hunter will mistake you for prey. Still, you want to be careful if you're camping and exploring in an area that's popular with hunters and it's hunting season. Check online or ask locally about hunting seasons. If it is hunting season, wear bright colors and be watching for hunters, and also be vigilant if you hike cross-country, especially in dense forest or brush.

Bears

Bears come in two varieties in North America. The far more common black bear frequents large parts of the mountainous West, the Mid-Atlantic States, New England, other areas of the United States, and much of Canada and Alaska. The grizzly bear (brown bear) inhabits parts of Montana and Wyoming, and much of western Canada and Alaska.

The best way to keep bears out of your camp is to eliminate all scents that attract them. Food, including garbage and dirty dishes, tops the list, but numerous odors intrigue bears, including toothpaste, lotions, and cosmetics. So make sure that anything that emits odors is stored in your vehicle in airtight containers like coolers, or is tightly wrapped in multiple plastic bags. Be aware that bears are especially attracted to the smell of cooked meat (bacon maybe most of all).

If you sleep in a tent, make sure there is no food or other scented items in the tent with you, nor any clothes you wore while cooking. Locate your tent as far as possible upwind of both your vehicle and the place where you cook.

Bears rarely confront humans; they will usually turn tail and run. If one approaches your campsite, you can try to scare it away by shouting or banging pots and pans. If that doesn't work, get in your vehicle, or if you can't do that, follow the advice below.

If you're hiking or otherwise exploring away from your campsite, make noise, especially in grizzly country; this will give the bear time to notice you and get out of the way. Always be watching your surroundings and avoid getting between a mother bear and a cub.

What should you do if you see a bear? If it hasn't seen you, back away and go a different route. If it has seen you, face the bear, speak calmly, move your arms slowly from your sides to a horizontal position, and avoid direct eye contact. If you have bear spray with you, now's the time to have it in your hand, ready for use. If the bear shows no obvious interest, began backing away slowly while still facing the bear, until you are a long distance away.

But what if the bear moves toward you? Stay as calm as you can with your arms horizontal. When the bear stops, start backing away. If the bear again moves toward you, stop again. Repeat until the bear loses interest.

And if the bear moves toward you and you sense an attack coming? Yell, act aggressively, and use bear spray, if you have it. Advice diverges on actual attacks, depending on the species. If it's a grizzly bear, lay flat on the ground on your stomach, with your hands protecting your head, and play dead. If the bear tries to roll you over, continue rolling back onto your stomach. Wait until you're sure the bear is gone before moving.

By contrast, if a black bear attacks you, fight back with all you've got, concentrating on the face and muzzle.

Keep in mind that bear attacks are very rare, given how often people encounter the creatures. I've probably seen 50 or so bears in my life, and not once did one act in a threatening manner. Nearly all of them ran away, and quickly.

And speaking of running, you can't outrun a bear, so don't even try.

Mountain Lions

Mountain lions (cougars, pumas) have an extensive range in the western portion of North America. Mountain lions almost always avoid humans. The odds are very low that you'll ever see one, although the odds are high that one will see you, if you get out into the wild much.

In general, keep children and pets close to you. If you do see a mountain lion, first pick up any small children and leash any dogs. Then shout and extend your arms in a threatening manner. If convenient, also throw rocks. If you have bear spray, get it out and be ready to use it. If attacked by a mountain lion you must fight back with all your strength and courage. As with bears, dogs can attract mountain lions.

Other Large Mammals

Most large mammals won't bother you, especially if you follow the "rule of thumb" to make sure you keep a proper distance, as discussed in "Chapter Six: Dispersed Camping Best Practices." Just don't get too close, especially if animals have young ones nearby.

Snakes

Poisonous snakes exist throughout most of North America, with the many species of rattlesnake the most pervasive. The best way to avoid snake bite is to always watch where you place your feet and hands. If you do get bit by a rattlesnake or other poisonous snake, stay calm and get to a hospital as soon as you can.

Personal Protection

Some people want protection when they're out in back-country, and I respect that.

The biggest question: should you take a gun? This is up to your personal philosophy and assessment of potential risks. If you do take a gun, I strongly advise you to follow the law for the area you'll be exploring. Also make sure you have the proper training and that you follow best practices for gun safety.

Pepper spray is another option. Bear spray is designed primarily to work on bears (and also mountain lions) and is often prohibited for use against humans. However, you can purchase a small canister of pepper spray that easily fits in your pocket that is designed to be used against a human that is attacking you or threatening imminent attack.

Pepper spray is inexpensive, easy to use, and doesn't cause permanent harm. Bear spray can be quite effective (studies show it's more effective than firearms against bears). Pepper spray for human attackers can also be very effective.

Knives are quite popular in the backcountry and have many uses besides protection. Just follow any regulations.

If you are ever in a situation in the backcountry or elsewhere that makes you feel unsafe, leave and go someplace safer.

Exploring

You'll likely want to explore the area near your dispersed camping site. Indeed, this may be the main reason you're out there. You might walk dirt roads, hike trails or cross-country, go mountain biking, or explore with a motorcycle or other motorized vehicle.

The key point: don't get lost!

Make sure you have maps and apps, plus good advice from agency personnel and guidebooks. And follow the advice in "Chapter Five: Finding the Best Dispersed Camping Sites" for not getting lost when traveling backroads in your vehicle, applied here to your method of movement. Take detailed notes, either verbal on a recording device like your phone, or with pen on paper, of how far you went, and which direction you turned on which trail or road. Take pictures of junctions to jog your memory.

Take the Ten Essentials

Mountaineers Books, the publisher of my Northern California hiking guidebooks, first presented the Ten Essentials in the third edition of their classic *Mountaineering: The Freedom of the Hills.* It's golden advice for whenever and wherever you head out into the wild. Here is the latest version of what you need with you:

1. Navigation (map and compass)
2. Sun protection (hat, sunglasses, and sunscreen)
3. Insulation (extra clothing)
4. Illumination (headlamp or flashlight)
5. First-aid supplies
6. Fire (fire starter and matches/lighter)
7. Repair kit and tools (including knife)
8. Nutrition (extra food)
9. Hydration (extra water)
10. Emergency shelter

You also want to take your cell phone (but don't count on getting reception) and/or a satellite phone, plus an emergency signaling device or two, like a whistle, mirror, or brightly colored piece of cloth or plastic.

Whenever I do a more remote hike with few or no people around, I always go prepared to spend the night—an uncomfortable and perhaps chilly night, but one where I'll be dry, non-hypothermic, and hydrated and fed the next morning.

Keeping Your Dogs Safe

Many of you travel with dogs. I did the same with my two golden retrievers Hana and Molly for many years. Here are key considerations to minimize the probability of problems for your pooches.

1. Be careful letting them roam off-leash. I get that you may want to do this (and I often did), but first be sure your dog isn't the type to wander off. Losing a dog in the backcountry can easily be a permanent loss. If you're not sure, test how they do near to home, where if they do get lost, you'll likely get them back again. A collar and a tag with your phone number, and also a microchip, make it easier for someone to return your dog if it gets lost.

2. Be watchful of wildlife interactions. As I discuss in "Chapter Six: Dispersed Camping Best Practices," dogs can scare away wildlife and interfere with their feeding and other habits. Wildlife can also be dangerous. My dogs were attacked by porcupines and sprayed by skunks. They also once chased a black bear which, thankfully, just hightailed it away rather than turning and confronting them. And as stated above, dogs can actually lead bears and mountain lions to you.

3. Bring a first aid kit for your dog. These are available at pet supply stores and online.

4. Watch for insect problems. This can range from ticks to bites. Molly once got bit on the nose by some insect when we were camped in Kofa Wildlife Refuge in southwestern Arizona; her face swelled up dramatically and I initially feared for her life.

5. Prickly plants can also be an issue. Be especially wary in the desert with cactus, including those that grow low on the ground that dogs can step on. Needle-nose pliers are useful for extracting spines.

My Story: Hana and Molly Find the Way Back

My most extensive stint of dispersed camping occurred in 1999 and 2000 in my (mostly) trusty Ford Econoline van, always accompanied by (mostly) trusty canine sidekicks, golden retrievers Hana and Molly.

Hana (left) and Molly: they loved exploring outside!

In May of 1999 we were exploring southern Utah just west of Bryce Canyon National Park. We'd driven a ways south down a major dirt road in Dixie National Forest, and then taken a decent side road a couple of miles to a good camping spot.

Late one afternoon we headed out for a hike, utilizing a network of lesser dirt roads. The plan was to reach a point high enough and open enough that I could find cell reception and call a friend to wish him happy birthday. Our last major turn occurred after we'd climbed a rough animal path from one dirt road up to another, and then turned left. At the time I made special note of a distinctive dead tree with a twisted trunk beside this junction, so that I'd know where we needed to go right and descend on the return journey.

We headed farther uphill and westerly, and eventually did find a spot with beautiful open vista of forest punctuated by the same sherbet orange sandstone formation for which Bryce Canyon National Park is so famous. I made my call and then spent time taking in the majesty of the panorama.

By now it's near sunset and we're a couple of miles from the car. We begin walking back, with the girls 50 feet or so ahead. I was paying attention, thinking about the turn to the right by the distinctive dead tree, but I was also, of course, thinking many other thoughts.

I round a bend on the dirt road and see Hana and Molly stopped at the distinctive dead tree, bodies pointed downhill in the direction we need to go, both looking at me expectantly. I think they realized darkness was close and that we were in new territory, and they wanted to get back to the van (and supper). Down we went, back to the van (and supper).

Lessons Learned

1. Always pay attention to all junctions when exploring, especially when you don't have a good map and are just winging it.

2. It's important to identify visual cues to remind you of junctions and orientation in general, in this case the distinctive dead tree.

3. Sometimes (and only sometimes!) your dogs will know the way back. Read on...

My Story: Hana and Molly DON'T Find the Way Back

First off, it wasn't their fault. I was responsible for all navigation, and they usually just followed me wherever I went.

It's May of 2000 and the girls and I have found yet another kick-ass dispersed camping spot, this time along a narrow dirt road off Spencer Flat Road, itself off Highway 12 in Utah's Grand Staircase-Escalante National Monument. Just before sunset we walked downslope and about 400 yards away from the van to an open area with a spectacular view of the sculpted red sandstone formations of the Escalante River, one of my favorite places on the planet.

We watch the interplay of light and shadow as the sun approached the horizon, and then the attenuation of color as shadows fill the landscape. About 40 minutes after sunset, as Venus and the first bright stars appear in the sky, we start walking back to the van.

Now, I had paid attention to where the van was and where we were; several times as we walked down to our viewpoint, I had turned around to note landmarks so I would have the correct direction and distance.

But alas, I did not do it well enough! We walked back in the gathering dark, but when we got to where I expected the van to be, it was not there. Worse, with all the juniper trees and the growing darkness, I could not see very far at all.

Initially I wasn't worried. I walked in a spiral around the area where I thought the van should be, but I couldn't find it. Alarmed, I headed partially back down to where we'd watched the sunset so I could again walk up using my earlier bearings. But we got the same result: no van.

I briefly searched a bit more where I thought it should be, but no luck. Now I'm really worried. I know no one stole the van; I just can't find it. And it's nearly dark with no moon.

I stop and think about the best course of action. I'm dressed in pants, a t-shirt, and a sweatshirt. We can survive a night in the dark, but it would be very unpleasant.

So I develop a plan. Get back to Spencer Flat Road, know which direction to turn to find the dirt road I parked on, and then walk that dirt road until I find the van.

By now it's almost completely dark. We head about 200 yards through the juniper and sagebrush in the direction of Highway 12, parallel to Spencer Flat Road. We then turn left and I lope carefully directly toward Spencer Flat Road, making sure I don't trip or run into vegetation. The goal is to get to Spencer Flat Road before all twilight is gone.

Thankfully we do reach Spencer Flat Road with no problems. This is important, because there's a possibility other people could be driving the road and could help us. Also, the road is wide and flat and fairly easy to walk, even though it was now completely dark.

We were very fortunate that it was a clear night. You may not know it, but you can see a bit by starlight, and luckily Venus was also in the sky. I could faintly make out the road bed as we walked along, and I kept my eyes glued to the left edge, hoping I would see the secondary road we'd camped on.

And, soon enough, I was barely able to make out a secondary dirt road. Still not entirely sure it was actually ours, we headed down it while I was extra careful with my footing. And... after a few hundred yards we came upon the van. Such relief, such joy!

Lessons Learned

1. Always, always pay attention to where you are and where your vehicle is! This was pre-GPS days, but now you can use your phone and an app to mark the location of your vehicle and then use the app to help you navigate the way back.

Mind you, don't count on the app. Use all the other tools and methods I detail in this chapter.

2. Be especially careful about heading out to explore late in the day, particularly if you plan to come back after sunset.

3. Always take the Ten Essentials mentioned above, even if you think there's no way you can get stuck out away from your vehicle after dark. For example, a headlamp or flashlight will help you find your way, and the other items of the Ten Essentials will help keep you warm, fed, and hydrated.

Chapter Eight

Sleep for Free in Towns and Cities

This is not my area of expertise, because even when I was living and traveling in a van for months at a time, I was nearly always able to find legal places for dispersed camping on government land, or I stayed at the home of a friend or family member. However, I know many people who do frequently sleep in their vehicles in and near towns, or near major roads, so I've solicited their advice and combined that with information gleaned from government officials, print sources, and the Internet.

So You Want to Sleep for Free...

Probably because you're on your way to the backcountry to do dispersed camping, but it's a long ways away and you can't make it in one day. Or maybe in your travels you do a combination of dispersed camping and occasionally like to hang out near towns. There are definitely options for sleeping for free in and near towns, and for most of them you'll need a vehicle to sleep in.

Friends and Family

This is the best option and the one I have typically used, especially when I was living in my van long-term. I spent most of my time in Northern California where I was born and raised, so I was able to spend a night or three in many places, which always included a welcome shower and the ability to do a load of laundry, plus the chance to visit with loved ones.

Couch Surfing

Couch surfing—staying at peoples' homes, often on the couch—has grown tremendously in popularity in recent years. It can be a great way to meet cool people and learn about new places. CouchSurfing.com is a popular website for the activity. Many people who offer their homes prefer to do so to people who have opened their own homes to others in the past. Since you're essentially dealing with strangers, do be careful, especially if you are a woman.

Sleeping at City-Approved Sites

More towns and cities are approving designated areas for people to sleep overnight in their vehicles. Usually the number of allowed vehicles is limited, often severely so. The programs are designed primarily to help local homeless people, not specifically folks who aren't homeless but are just traveling through or visiting for a short time. Search online for the specific city department handling the program and give a call, or, if that fails, call the main information number for the city. You may also get information from social media, like local Facebook groups for the city.

Careful!

In many of the following options, sleeping overnight in your vehicle is often prohibited. Under no circumstances do I advise you to do something against the law. In each specific case you need to make sure that sleeping overnight is legal: check online, but also call the specific business, city government, or law enforcement agency (nonemergency number = NOT 911).

Check dispersedcamping.net for websites that share information about specific places you can legally sleep overnight.

Business Parking Lots

If you stay overnight in your self-contained vehicle in the parking lot of a business, don't set up your chairs, barbecue, etc. Park near the outer edges far away from the entrances and delivery truck routes. Stay inside your vehicle for the most part, only stay one night, leave fairly early in the morning, and definitely consider shopping at the store.

Wal-Mart

Some Wal-Mart stores allow travelers to spend the night. It has to be allowed by the local government, and the individual store has to approve it.

Big Box Stores

You may be able to legally park overnight at some stores, including Cabela's and others. Always call first and ask the manager.

Casinos

Many casinos welcome RVs to stay in their parking lots. Always check first.

Truck Stops

Truck stops frequently allow RVs and vans to stay overnight. Again, ask first. Some truckers resent RVs taking up space in crowded lots, so be sensitive to this.

Rest Areas

This is usually a long shot because many states and local governments prohibit sleeping overnight at rest areas along interstate highways. However, it doesn't hurt to call the local police (often the county sheriff) to ask.

Sleeping on Residential Streets

I don't recommend this. It's frequently against city rules, and many of the people in residential areas don't want people sleeping in vehicles on their streets. Check with the city government for rules and ask locally for recommendations.

If it is legal, make sure you scout your spot well before bedtime. Look for a place on a quiet, mostly level street, hopefully away from houses. Show up just before you want to sleep, and then go straight to bed, making no noise and showing no light. Set an alarm to get up early and get out of there. It's best to not exit your vehicle at all.

Sleeping Along Highways

Rural highways and other roads often have pullouts with room for you to park your rig. Frequently, overnight parking is prohibited (look for a sign), but if it's not, this a decent option. The downsides are lack of privacy and the noise and lights of passing vehicles.

My Story: Sleeping Alongside Highway 101 in Northern California

For many years Redwood National & State Parks in Northern California allowed people to sleep for free in RVs and other vehicles alongside a stretch of U.S. Highway 101 bordering a broad beach in Humboldt County. Legal dispersed camping sites are almost non-existent in this area, so this was a popular spot. (Note the term "was": overnight parking is no longer allowed here.)

One summer night in 2000, while traveling with my golden retrievers Hana and Molly in the Econoline van on our way from the Crescent City area to explore Arcata, I was desperate for a legal place to sleep for free. So, even though it went strongly against my nature to sleep beside a busy highway, I parked alongside 101, in line with dozens of other vehicles, mostly RVs but also a few vans.

It sucked! Every few minutes—all night long!—a vehicle went whizzing by, often a roaring diesel truck. Unfortunately, I had not set up my van to block all light, so I also had to deal with bright headlights illuminating my sleeping space.

Lessons Learned

1. Avoid sleeping beside a busy road if at all possible.

2. If you must sleep by a road, block all your windows from outside light. (And consider a sleep mask if you can't.)

3. Traffic noise can definitely interfere with sleep. I now have a white-noise phone app that helps drown out extraneous sounds.

Our Story: Sleeping Alongside Highway 50 in Nevada

May 2019: Stephanie and I are making our way back to our home in Ashland, Oregon, near the end of a fantastic three-week trip to southern Utah, on the maiden voyage of the Kia Sedona.

Stormy weather on Highway 50

Highway 50, the "Loneliest Road in America," is one of my absolute favorite highways in the United States. It rolls through vast stretches of empty country in the Basin and Range of Nevada and western Utah, alternating between jagged mountain ranges rising above 10,000 feet and broad, open basins several thousand feet lower.

There's a lot of government land along Highway 50, and we'd found an excellent campsite in western Utah the night before, just an easy half-mile up an excellent dirt road in one of the mountain ranges.

Our great campsite the first night

Now it's the next day, a day with periods of heavy rain. We have plans to stay with friends in Reno the following night, but we still need to find a place to sleep tonight. We're loving the interplay of dark rainclouds, intermittent sunbeams, and the vivid landscape of Nevada, and we stop several times to take short walks and enjoy the beauty.

So, when you travel as a couple, you make decisions as a couple. About an hour before sunset, we crossed yet another range, one obviously marked as BLM land, with multiple dirt roads that we could explore to find a camping spot. I wanted to stop right then; however, Stephanie wanted to push on and log more driving miles on 50 before finding a site. I lost!

I figured that we'd be able to find good dirt roads on government land in the next "range," but no luck. So we drop down into the next basin to the west, where I hope we'll find both signs identifying government land and also a good dirt road to access it.

Well, we do find a dirt road, but it's not obvious whether it's government land or private land. It's sunset now, and we're feeling pressured to settle in. We take the dirt road and drive for several miles. I choose a likely looking side road, but it ends near a corral in an area that's really mucky from the recent rains. We decide this is not the place for us, in part because we're not sure if it's government land or private land, and also because we're concerned that more rains overnight could make the road impassable the next morning.

So we go back to Highway 50 and continue driving west, now in total darkness. As mentioned in "Chapter Five: How to Find the Best Dispersed Camping Sites," you don't want to be looking for a camping spot in the dark. But there we were.

As we topped out on the next range west, we spotted a short dirt road on the right that paralleled 50. I quickly braked and turned onto the road, which led to a small parking area about 200 feet from the highway. Desperate, we decided to overnight there. I positioned the van so it was level and as far away from the road as possible.

We were both concerned about being woken up by the intermittent traffic. However, we both managed to sleep quite well. Being the "Loneliest Road in America" meant very little traffic in the wee hours of the night, and we were far enough off the road that the occasional light and noise was minimal.

Lessons Learned

1. Better to start searching for your site earlier than later!

2. Be careful of muddy roads after rains and pay attention to upcoming storms that can worsen road conditions.

3. Deciding when to start looking for a spot and choosing the actual spot are joint decisions when traveling with others.

4. Highway 50 has very little traffic at night.

Appendix: What to Take

This appendix includes the gear and supplies most people need for dispersed camping. Adapt it to create a list of exactly what you need.

On dispersedcamping.net you'll find an online version of this list, along with my recommendations of the best specific products.

Also see dispersedcamping.net for recommendations of:

-- Books
-- Maps
-- Apps
-- Websites
-- And more!

Eating and Drinking

Cooler
Ice
Storage bins
Water
Water bottles
Water purification
Food
Cooking oil
Salt and pepper
Spices

Condiments
Coffee/tea
Stove
Fuel
Lighter/matches
Mugs
Cups
Plates
Bowls
Forks
Spoons
Knives
Cutting board
Pots and pans
Potholder
Spatula
Stirring spoon
Dish soap, biodegradable
Scrubber/sponge
Dish towel
Paper towels
Can opener
Corkscrew/bottle opener
Storage containers
Aluminum foil
Napkins
Plastic storage bags
Garbage bags
Spray bottle of water

Sleeping

Sleeping bags
Blankets
Sleeping pads
Pillows
Sheets/pillowcases
Tent
Ground cloth/tarp

Clothing

Hat
Knit cap
Sunglasses
Gloves: warm
Gloves: work
Shirts: short-sleeve
Shirts: long-sleeve
Sweaters
Sweatshirts
Jackets/fleece
Pants
Shorts
Underwear
Swimsuit
Shoes and/or boots
Socks
Sandals
Flip-flops
Raingear/umbrella
Sewing kit

Health and Safety

First aid kit
Head lamp
Fire extinguisher: multipurpose

Personal Items

Medicines
Vitamins/supplements
Glasses/contacts
Toothbrush and toothpaste
Floss
Deodorant
Skin lotion
Lip balm
Sunblock
Body soap, biodegradable
Shampoo, biodegradable
Comb/brush
Shaving supplies
Body towel
Hand towel
Fingernail and toenail clippers
Toilet paper
Hand sanitizer
Birth control
Feminine products
Portable camp shower
Eye mask
Ear plugs
N95 mask for wildfire smoke

Outdoor Gear

Folding chairs
Folding table
Tablecloth
Sunshade
Umbrellas
Sitting pads
Headlamp/flashlight
Lantern
Hatchet
Fire starter
Insect repellent
Trowel/hand shovel
Clothesline and clothespins

Electronics

Cell phone
Cell phone charger
Satellite phone
SPOT device
Camera
Power charger
Batteries

Miscellaneous

Identification
Cash
Credit cards
Permits/licenses
Directions

Maps
Guidebooks
Road atlas

Multitool
Vehicle Repair Kit
Tire inflator
Battery charger
Duct tape
Rope/cord
Bungee cords
Scissors
Knife
Personal protection

Books
Binoculars
Music player
Ear buds
Cards/games
Notebook/pen
Musical instruments
Fishing gear

Dogs

Dog food and bowl
Dog water dish
Dog leash
Dog tether
Dog medicines
Dog first aid kit

Hiking/Exploring/Outdoors

Day pack
Navigation: maps, apps, compass
First aid kit
Knife
Headlamp
Sun protection
Extra clothes
Food
Water
Signaling device
Cell phone

About John Soares

From the time I was a young boy growing up in a rural area outside of Anderson, California, I spent as much time outside in nature as possible. Starting in my teen years, I began exploring the hiking trails in the mountains of Northern California. I expanded my wanderings to the entire western United States in early adulthood, which is also when I discovered the joys of dispersed camping.

After obtaining a bachelor's degree in biochemistry and a master's degree in political science from the University of California, Davis, I began a writing career for businesses and nonprofits that also included writing hiking guidebooks for Mountaineers Books, one of the world's premier publishers of outdoors titles. My current books include:

100 Classic Hikes: Northern California, fourth edition
Hike the Parks: Redwood National & State Parks
Day Hiking: Mount Shasta, Lassen & Trinity Alps Regions
Urban Trails: Sacramento

I've lived much of my life in rural areas and medium-sized and smaller towns in and near upper Northern California, including Redding, Chico, Crescent City, Mount Shasta, and Ashland, Oregon, where I currently live. I continue to write for a variety of clients as I enjoy life here in Ashland, and my sweetie Stephanie and I frequently hike, especially south of the border in the Mount Shasta area and nearby. Of course, we continue to take dispersed camping trips long and short, which we plan to do for the rest of our lives.

Find out more about me and my work online:

NorthernCaliforniaHikingTrails.com: Detailed information about my hiking guidebooks, plus extensive descriptions of hiking trails and advice on enjoying the outdoors safely

DispersedCamping.net: The main website for this book has an extensive list of resources, including recommendations on what to take, and also the latest information on dispersed camping in the United States.

JohnWrites.net: In my main writing work, I create a variety of content for businesses and nonprofits large and small, ranging from persuasive website copy to annual reports.

ProductiveWriters.com: I've been writing the Productive Writers blog since 2010. I offer a wide variety of advice to help writers be both more productive and more successful. I also sell the two ebooks I've written:

Find Your Freelance Writing Niches

Writing College Textbook Supplements: Developing Test Questions, Quiz Questions, Instructor Manuals, Lecture Outlines, and Other Curriculum Components, third edition

Acknowledgements

Many people helped make this a better book by sharing their knowledge of dispersed camping, by reading through the manuscript, or both. I'm especially grateful to the following people for their help:

-- Don Lee of the Mount Shasta Ranger Station
-- Nancy Soares, my sister-in-law
-- Jake Soares, my nephew

My siblings Eric Soares, Marc Soares, and Camille Soares-Brown, my father John Severin Soares, and my mother Mozelle Fitzhugh helped instill the love of the outdoors that led me to dispersed camping in the first place.

Jim Kakuk provided advice on the title and has always been an inspiration for adventuring in the wild.

And finally, my sweetheart Stephanie Hoffman read the entire manuscript and made several important suggestions. More importantly, she's given her full support throughout the entire project, and she's my main dispersed camping buddy.

Of course, any and all errors are entirely my responsibility.

Thank You! – And a Favor Request

My deepest thanks for purchasing *Camp for Free: Dispersed Camping & Boondocking on America's Public Lands*. I hope it inspires you to do more dispersed camping, and that it helps you get more enjoyment out of your time in the wild.

If you got value from this book, **please do me a big favor and review it on Amazon, Goodreads, your website, social media, and anywhere else you share reviews**.

Please also tell everyone you know who could be interested in dispersed camping about the book. Spread the word!

Boondocking Notebook/Journal

Record all the key data and save all your important memories for all your boondocking and dispersed camping adventures.

Get the details on Amazon by searching for the exact title, or title keywords along with "John Soares" (and click the cover to "Look Inside.")

More From Get Outside Press

Get Outside Press (GetOutsidePress.com) features an expanding series of books to help you get outside and enjoy the outdoors. **Find them on Amazon** by searching for the exact title, or title keywords along with the author's name (John Soares).

Made in the USA
Middletown, DE
10 February 2022